5/14/07

To

Mark —

Best Wishes —

Ed. Whymper

Stealing
Your
Life

Also by Frank W. Abagnale

The Art of the Steal

Catch Me If You Can

Stealing
Your
Life

The Ultimate
Identity Theft
Prevention Plan

Frank W. Abagnale

Broadway Books

New York

BROADWAY

PUBLISHED BY BROADWAY BOOKS

Published in the United States by Broadway Books, an imprint of The Doubleday Broadway Publishing Group, a division of Random House, Inc., New York. www.broadwaybooks.com

BROADWAY BOOKS and its logo, a letter B bisected on the diagonal, are trademarks of Random House, Inc.

This title may be purchased for business or promotional use or for special sales. For information, please write to: Special Markets Department, Random House, Inc., 1745 Broadway, MD 6-3, New York, NY 10019, or specialmarkets@randomhouse.com.

This book is designed to provide accurate and authoritative information on the subject of the prevention of identity theft. It is sold with the understanding that neither the Author nor the Publisher is engaged in rendering legal, accounting, or other professional services by publishing this book. As each individual situation is unique, questions relevant to the prevention of identity theft and specific to the individual should be addressed to an appropriate professional to ensure that the situation has been evaluated carefully and appropriately. The Author and Publisher specifically disclaim any liability, loss, or risk that is incurred as a consequence, directly or indirectly, of the use and application of any contents of this work.

Book design by Donna Sinisgalli

Library of Congress Cataloging-in-Publication Data
Abagnale, Frank W., 1948–
Stealing your life : the ultimate identity theft prevention plan / Frank W. Abagnale.—1st ed.
p.   cm.
1. Identity theft—United States. 2. Identity theft—United States—Prevention. I. Title.

HV6684.U6A23 2006
362.88—dc22
2006013918

ISBN 978-0-7679-2586-0

PRINTED IN THE UNITED STATES OF AMERICA

1 3 5 7 9 10 8 6 4 2

First Edition

In memory of

Joseph G. Shea

**Special Agent, Federal Bureau
of Investigation**

(Carl Hanratty)

Contents

Stealing
Your
Life

1

The Sweetest Con of All

Anthony Dwight Stone was perfectly happy being Anthony Dwight Stone, for all of his first thirty-one years. This sense of contentment continued right up until the day, a few years ago, when he learned that Thomas Earl Batts had decided to also become Anthony Dwight Stone, and the world got a little too crowded.

The real Anthony Stone was driving through Nash County, North Carolina, when he was stopped for speeding. When his license was inspected, the police gave him the news that he was wanted for drug possession. Geez, he said, they had to be kidding. They weren't, and he got tossed in jail for the night. Then the police showed him a picture that was supposedly him. It was of a man with his hair coiled in braids and a stomach that ran on forever who easily weighed three hundred pounds; Stone boasted curly hair and weighed 170, tops. He recognized the man right away. That was Thomas Earl Batts, his sister's boyfriend.

Being his sister's boyfriend had made it pretty easy for Batts to gather the necessary information—Social Security number and a few other key facts—and slip into Anthony Stone's identity. And it certainly changed Anthony Stone's view of what sisters are for.

As it turned out, Stone said, Batts had quietly appropriated Stone's identity some ten years earlier and had been living right alongside him, using credit cards in Stone's name to buy various necessary and unnecessary merchandise. He had gone and gotten a loan in Stone's name to purchase a house. And out of force of bad habit, he had built up a tidy little rap sheet.

None of this was a good thing for Anthony Stone. Batts, for instance, didn't bother to keep current with his credit. But then, what did he care? He wasn't really Anthony Stone. And so the real Anthony Stone found himself branded as a congenital loser. He had an impossible time getting credit—any credit. "Doors of all kinds were shut in my face," he said. He'd apply for a job and would be promptly turned down; one time he found work and, after a lagging credit check, was whisked right out of a company car.

When he belatedly got around to applying to college, he got nothing but rejections, since his sketchy credit and criminal misdeeds weren't quite what the admissions people had in mind for their incoming class. It didn't seem to matter that it wasn't his credit record or his criminal record. "I'd get into my apartment and get a notice six or seven times that I was evicted," he said. "I felt like life had stopped."

It took years to untangle the mess. And Anthony Stone had to wonder, what if it happened again? Which is why he went to court and changed his name to Stone Tyler, essentially ceding his old identity to the dustbin. At the same time, he applied for a new Social Security number. He was laughed at and told it couldn't be done, but he ultimately did get it done. "Basically, you can't get your Social Security number changed unless it's life-threatening," he said.

Tyler, who lives in Durham, North Carolina, at last got into college and found a job with Blue Cross Blue Shield. Batts served a brief jail sentence, and that was it. For many people, the metamorphosis that Stone Tyler chose—new name, new Social Security number—might seem like an extreme response to an admittedly awful situation, and I wouldn't recommend going quite that far. But from where he sat he saw no choice. This con was just too much for him.

His rude ordeal taught this young man, who had been leading an unremarkable life in North Carolina, that he lived in a new world in which all identities are at risk and, in essence, are in play.

I know cons, and right away I saw that this one was going to be the sweetest of all. For the past thirty-two years, ever since forsaking my foolish teenage infatuation with perpetrating swindles, I've been a professional expert in how to prevent fraud. Nearly twenty years ago, as I was busy trying to help banks and businesses stop the spiraling increase in rubber checks and wily embezzlement schemes, it became obvious to me that a brand-new fraud, still in its formative stages and without even a clarifying name, was destined to overwhelm all the others as the clear crime of choice. In fact, it was a crook's dream come true, the sort of surefire caper that makes a career criminal glad he ignored his mother's advice and picked the wrong side of the law.

Years before, I would never have guessed that it could even be invented, for it was the most incredible but also the simplest crime ever perpetrated. And if I manage to live forty more years, it will remain the simplest crime ever committed—and the most profitable.

This festering crime is what we now know as identity theft, the wholesale lifting of someone's identity for illicit gain. It's stealing that identity, then using it to access a person's bank account, their personal information, and their personal finances. It's becoming someone else for the bucks.

Why did I think it contained such enormous promise for thieves? First of all, it is elementary to pull off. If you have my name, my date of birth, and my Social Security number, that's pretty much all you need in order to become me. It takes very little investment capital. A phone and a cheap computer will get you started. If you want to write phony checks, you'll need a few vital tools like a blow-dryer, cake pans, and a common household chemical. You can pick them up at your nearest discount drugstore, and no one will be the wiser.

Then, the rewards are enormous. Identity theft will afford you access not only to someone's wallet and bank account but to his very life and character, his entire ability to borrow and spend. Are you worried about the law? No need. Technology has made identity theft easy to execute behind the shadowy cloak of a computer keyboard. You don't even have to be in the same city, or country, as your victim. You can steal someone's identity without being able to speak his language or pronounce her name.

Moreover, law enforcement cares less about identity theft than it does about double-parked cars and public loiterers. Your chances of getting caught are minuscule. But even if you do get caught, you are unlikely to spend a single night in jail. Swiping a kid's bike might have graver consequences.

When I ran all these things through my mind, they unnerved

me to no end. And my long-dormant criminal instincts stirred a little and made me think, Why didn't they invent this con back when
I could have used it?

When I was passing phony checks in other people's names more
than thirty years ago, for example, it took me three months and a
million-dollar Heidelberg printing press to create and cash a realistic-
looking product. Today criminals do it in an instant on a $500 com-
puter, with no witnesses to pick them out in a lineup, because they're
doing it from an armchair in China or Russia, a continent away. And
checks are simply one piece of an identity thief's arsenal.

In recent years identity theft has become the very monster I
feared it would become. It's a crime so versatile that the list of potential targets is endless. Who's at risk? Anyone who has a credit card
or a bank account, or who pays a bill. Anyone who has a mortgage, a
car loan, or a debit card. Anyone who has a driver's license, a Social
Security number, or a job. Anyone who has phone service or health
insurance. Anyone who goes on the Internet.

Even somebody who's always watching his back, like me. People of all ages, all races, all incomes, and both sexes. A thirty-five-
year-old New York busboy had the hubris to choose names off the
Forbes 400 list, including Ross Perot, Oprah Winfrey, Michael
Bloomberg, and Ted Turner, gleaned additional information on
them from the Internet, and became them. Robert De Niro's identity was assumed by his movie double. Tiger Woods was victimized
by a California man who rented a moving truck and a storage locker
in his name. In Chandler, Arizona, the identity of the retired police
chief was taken over by a woman who loaded up at Wal-Mart and
Sam's Club stores. Twin brothers were kicked off the popular *American Idol* show after police said they had bought a car using the
stolen identities of two unwitting fans.

In other words, anyone who's alive is a potential victim. Actually, I stand corrected—even the dead can become targets of this insidious crime. You can have lived your life, then be resting eternally six feet under—and you're still not protected from the long reach of identity thieves. Scam artists have no compunction. After all, the dead rarely complain.

These days you can't go to a party or have lunch with three or four people without someone in that group mentioning that he got a phony e-mail, or that his credit card was compromised—that somehow someone snatched his identity. Identity theft is the fastest-growing criminal activity in the country (and it's doing awfully well abroad). And it could be coming soon to a bank account near you.

Every Four Seconds

Accurate statistics on identity theft are tricky to come by because it remains an underdocumented crime. Many people and businesses don't report incidents to the police, and a startling number of people don't even know their identities have been stolen. The reported numbers, though, are shocking.

At the time when I wrote my last book, *The Art of the Steal,* in 2001, there were about 750,000 documented victims of identity theft, and losses to banks and credit card companies amounted to $5 billion. That's not chicken feed, but in 2003 the Federal Trade Commission released the most exhaustive government study to date of identity theft, estimating that there had been 27.3 million victims in the prior five years. In 2004 alone, around 10 million consumers suffered from some variation of identity theft, and losses exceeded $54 billion. In 2005 the FTC was swamped with five thousand calls a week related to the problem, more than they got on any other issue and triple what they had received just five years before.

When a major insurance company recently polled a sizable sampling of its policyholders on their biggest fears, the number-one response was their fear of losing all their assets through bad stock market and other investments. Number two was their fear of identity theft. Throughout the country people go out of their way to put multiple locks on their doors and install costly silent alarm systems. Well, in a given year, about 2.6 percent of Americans have their homes burglarized, but about 4.3 percent of them have their identities stolen. In 2005 it's believed that an identity was stolen every four seconds.

The crime has universal appeal to criminals, and it's happening all over the world. A recent survey conducted in New Zealand by Baycorp Advantage found that one in ten of the 450 Kiwis questioned said that they had been the victim of identity theft.

The crime has become so mainstream that comedians have begun joking about it, always a tip-off that it's time to worry. Andy Borowitz, a humor columnist, quipped recently that a thief who rounded up a half-million identities returned all but four of them because the other 499,996 were "totally worthless." Identity thieves, he said, were getting awfully sick of this, feeling it only fair that financial institutions clearly flag deadbeat identities so that crooks don't have to waste their valuable time.

I'll Tell You Twenty-two Things Overnight

In my entire career I have never encountered a crime as easy to pull off as identity theft. The main reason is that so much personal information is widely and publicly available, there for anyone to take. Once upon a time criminals used to have to really work to make an illegal living. Back when I was passing bad checks, if you wanted to lift information on someone's identity, you had to penetrate so much bureaucracy that it almost wasn't worth the headache. You had to go down to the county records department and try to cadge information, or try to get at boating records and mortgage information by cajoling low-level civil service workers. It could be done, but it took know-how and talent, plus you had to do it in person, producing witnesses. Now rank amateurs can do it, with technology's helping hand. An identity thief can acquire everything needed to steal your life by going online for less than thirty minutes. If he's in a big rush and has a high-speed Internet hookup, fifteen might suffice. Getting someone's supposedly secure information is no harder than downloading a Paris Hilton video.

I regularly teach agents at the FBI Academy, and one little demonstration I do is to ask one of my students for his address. Nothing more, not even his name. By the following morning I'm able to hand over to him twenty-two pieces of so-called "private" information about him, including his Social Security number, birth date, salary, current bank and account numbers, mother's maiden name, children's names, spouse's name and Social Security number, and neighbors. I can even reveal who lives with him in his house but isn't related to him. And I don't even have to do something as dramatic as hack into a bank database. All this information is readily available from publicly accessible sources on the Internet, and you or Joe Criminal can get it as easily as I did. Imagine how much I could have found out about the guy if I had decided to break the law!

Just this past year a friend of mine had his birthday in June, and I wanted to send him a card, but I couldn't remember the exact date. So I logged on to the Web and went to the Texas Public Health Records, because I knew he had been born in Texas, and typed in his name. Up came the city and county he was born in, as well as his mother's maiden name, his date of birth, and on and on, all the information right there online for free.

Consider these sobering facts:

* Six out of ten American companies and government agencies have already been hacked.
* An estimated 80 percent of birth certificate requests are fulfilled through the mail for people using only a name and a return address. So I could take your name, use my address, and get your birth certificate. From there I'm off to the races.
* Americans write 39 billion checks a year, and half of these folks never reconcile their bank statements.
* A Social Security number costs $49 on the black market. A driver's license goes for $90. A birth certificate will set you back $79.

In today's hotly competitive financial marketplace, speed is of the essence. Thieves love fast credit approval, because haste is the enemy of accuracy. Credit card issuers, for their part, can be very sloppy in doling out cards, failing to match Social Security numbers and dates of birth and otherwise failing to take basic precautions in their eagerness to get cards in circulation. Issuers say their screening is tighter than ever, but dead people, one-year-old babies, and dogs of varying ages still find themselves offered preapproved cards. (I imagine a few turtles and some parakeets have gotten them as well.) A Livermore, California, man signed up for an e-mail account in his dog's name, expanding it to Clifford J. Dog. Sure enough, in short order Clifford got a preapproved credit card application. As a lark, the owner filled it out. Pugsy Malone was listed as the mother's name.

For the Social Security number, the owner chose 000-00-0000. Then he wrote that this was for a dog, please don't send a card. Naturally, the card came.

In fact, it's now child's play to assume someone's identity. Suppose you go to the grocery store and write a check for $52. The check bears your full name and address and maybe your phone number to boot. It also has the full name and address of the bank where the check is drawn and your account number. Maybe the clerk asks to see your driver's license. The clerk might jot down the license number (in nine states, that could still be your Social Security number) and even your date of birth.

Hundreds of people, from the grocery store clerk to check-clearing house employees, will see this check. Then it goes back to the payee bank. If you don't get your checks in your statement, they go to a company that shreds them—and even there they can be copied before being shredded. And that's just one way thieves can get virtually all the vital information they need.

To prove a point a few years ago, the California-based Foundation for Taxpayer and Consumer Rights went on the Internet and bought the Social Security numbers and home addresses of the CIA director, the attorney general, and the FTC chairman. It cost them $26. Sounds like a steal to me.

It's Even Working as You

Identity theft has differing definitions, for it comes in numerous guises, some significantly more serious than others. In its more limited forms, it can be as straightforward as getting hold of someone's credit card number, or the actual card, and using it illicitly. It can be copying a check and forging a person's signature on it. One thief used his stepfather's identity to buy tire rims on the Internet; another stole a Florida man's identity and wrote a bum check to a deli for $400 worth of hot dogs.

But it's the big stuff that goes well beyond tire rims that is most worrisome—full-blown identity theft, when a thief uses your personal information to fully inhabit your life. For not only has identity theft exploded in magnitude (as I feared it would), it has taken on dramatic new mutations. For instance, identity theft started years ago when a criminal could get enough information to apply for a Visa or MasterCard in someone's name. He'd use the card for two weeks, then throw it away. In those two weeks he'd run up the credit limit in frantic, nonstop spending (buying big-screen TVs, stereos, computers, the works), then destroy the card. A few weeks later the hapless victim would get a statement from the bank and would be left arguing, "I don't have a Visa card with Wells Fargo. I don't even have a big-screen TV."

Today, though, a criminal thinks, "If I can get a credit card in someone's name, then I can get a signature loan for twenty-five thousand dollars in their name. I'll buy a car. Buy a boat. Get a mortgage. I'll even work for somebody under contract labor and let the cardholder pay my taxes."

I've been teaching federal agents for over thirty years. When I started out, I taught counterfeiting and forgery, because those were the popular white-collar crimes that criminals used to fleece others. Today I teach e-commerce-related crimes that didn't exist back then, and I emphasize identity theft. I was teaching about phishing and pharming before those terms were coined. (We'll explore them later.) I ask new agents, Why would anyone rob a bank these days, which involves getting a gun and wearing a disguise and arranging for a getaway car, when you can clean out people's online banking accounts using your laptop while you watch NFL games?

Everything that you have access to, short of your own family, the identity thief masquerading as you has access to. It's a frightening prospect. Just ask anyone who's lived through the horror. You could literally find yourself dead, while your identity lives on. In Illinois a man being pursued for counterfeiting murdered a homeless man and snatched his identity, then faked his own death as a way to evade prosecution.

When a thief opens an entirely new account, as opposed to simply raiding or misusing an existing one, the per-victim dollar losses to both businesses and consumers are typically much steeper, and the time that's required to rectify the problem and restore the victim's credit standing tends to be lengthier. The FTC has estimated that when a crook simply uses a victim's established account, the loss to businesses averages $2,100 per victim, and the victim has to absorb very little direct loss. On the other hand, full-blown cases produce average losses to businesses of $10,200, with the individual being hit for $1,180.

One reason for the discrepancy is that raids on established accounts are likely to be detected more quickly, so the opportunity time for the criminal is briefer. But full-blown identity thieves tend to be appreciably more sophisticated. A crook who is crafty and sets up a new parallel life with plenty of cover can go on as your duplicate for years. I heard of a man who had lived under another person's identity for twenty-three years. Even his wife and children didn't know who he really was.

It's Even Bigger Than They Say

To be honest, I believe we still haven't even scratched the surface of this troubling social problem. Everyone, including the FTC, agrees that our current identity theft figures are undoubtedly low, because so many cases go unreported or undetected. Businesses commonly refrain from divulging them because they don't want unwanted bad publicity to tarnish their corporate identity or the impression to spread that they are not safeguarding their customers' personal information sufficiently. Studies show that lenders miscategorize a good deal of identity theft, often because it looks like delinquent bills rather than crime. Only months later, when the victim realizes what's been going on and complains, does it become apparent that fraud was involved. By then, the money has been written off as a credit loss.

Many consumers who are victimized don't inform the police or anyone else, because they're ashamed of what happened to them, especially when the culprit is someone they know, as is often the case. Many times the police won't do a report because the crime seems too trifling, or consumers are confused about what to do. The FTC study found that an astonishing 38 percent of victims never told a soul.

Still other thefts go unreported because their victims don't even realize what has happened. Identity theft is an invisible strike that is neither seen nor felt until long afterward. You know right away when you've been mugged or when your home has been burglarized, but you don't always know when your identity has been seized. It could be years and hundreds of thousands of lost dollars later before you find out the ugly truth. According to the FTC, the average victim doesn't realize that his identity has been stolen until thirteen months later. By that time the thief has moved on and assumed someone else's identity.

One of the scary things about identity theft is the extreme difficulty in determining who did it and how. When a crime remains unsolved, victims have no closure. According to the FTC survey, just about half of all victims had no idea *how* the perpetrator stole their identity. Indeed, they may never know, and that's an unnerving feeling to live with. Imagine that someone infiltrated your life, but you don't know who or how. All you can do is wonder.

It's Not My Problem—or Is It?

Despite the distressing statistics, far too many identity theft victims have the attitude that they aren't really victims at all. We have been told again and again that the real victims are the banks and credit card companies. It's true that these institutions do sometimes lose tens of thousands of dollars per incident. And it's true that most individuals don't end up directly paying for the fraudulent bills that are run up in their names.

But sometimes they do. Say a thief gets into your online banking bill-paying account and robs it. Of course you sit back and say, "Well, my bank must be liable for that." Is it? Did you read your deposit agreement? You signed it. I'm talking about that long legal-size paper, printed on both sides. In most cases the bank effectively says in that agreement that if you use XYZ Bank software and you bank with XYZ Bank online, then the bank assumes 100 percent liability; but if you use XYZ Bank online and you use Microsoft Money, Quicken, or some other software program, the bank assumes no liability. And indeed, why should it assume liability for something it has no control over? So the victims have to spend several years litigating in court, if they have enough money to afford a lawyer, to get their money back.

The FTC, in its study, found that while consumers may be protected from the bulk of the losses, they still suffered in 2002 to the tune of $5 billion.

Just because businesses are losing money, that doesn't mean that you aren't as well. Companies run up billions of dollars a year in losses from identity theft. Do they simply swallow it? Hardly. At the end of the year they take a 50 percent tax write-off, so the U.S. taxpayer picks up roughly half of their losses. The other half goes back into their operating budget and is reflected in increased prices, rates, fees, and service charges. In the end, you pay for everything.

Even if you don't lose money directly, getting debt collectors off your back and straightening out your tangled credit history is a horrific nightmare that will cost you not only time but money. A study by the Identity Theft Resource Center concluded that on average it takes a victim 330 hours (the range is from 3 hours to 5,840) and usually between $881 and $1,378 to get her credit report straightened out and her life back to normal. Fixing the problem is not as simple as saying, "That's not me." You have to prove that you didn't apply for that loan. You must convince the credit card or finance company that you didn't make those purchases. Then you must persuade all three credit bureaus that fraud was committed. In most cases the credit bureaus will refuse to delete the dispute from your credit file. Instead, they will put an asterisk next to the charge and say, "Customer disputes this Visa charge, claims they were a victim of identity theft." The result is that anyone who accesses your credit report, be it a potential employer or a company considering granting you credit, may question whether you really were a victim or if you were ripping somebody off. The crime leaves holes in people's lives.

Even after the theft has been stopped, victims are often denied loans, housing, and employment because of bad credit. When a twenty-two-year-old college student applied for an internship with the Department of Justice, a routine background check turned up the unexpected news that he was $45,000 in debt, courtesy of an identity thief. The scam had been going on since he was sixteen.

Try telling someone who has spent hundreds of hours (in many instances, years) clearing her name that she isn't a victim. I've heard countless firsthand stories of the traumatic emotional impact that identity theft inflicts on its victims and the strains it injects into relationships. A fire chief was arrested for trying to choke his wife during an argument. What caused him to lose his cool? The family had been under heavy stress because his wife had had her identity stolen and checks in her name were being passed all over town.

When someone else becomes you, the ransacking of your life is hard to cope with, and it inscribes scars on the soul. One victim said the experience was as if "a ghost has taken your soul. You don't know who it is, where they are, where they came from."

We'd Rather Get the Drug Dealers

Even though you hear a lot about identity theft these days, and prime-time TV commercials proudly tout the supposedly sophisticated measures various banks have instituted to repel it, the reality is that not nearly enough is being done to impede this crime. It remains very much a growth industry with dazzling future prospects. No one is giving you, the consumer, the true goods: that thieves have never had it easier and that authorities are pretty much clueless as to what to do about it.

Not surprisingly, a Gartner study found that identity thieves have something like a one-in-seven-hundred chance of getting caught by law enforcement. I've never met a criminal who wouldn't leap at those odds.

Too many people say they really don't care that a bank or credit card company lost $100,000 from identity theft—they consider it the company's problem. They're wrong. Identity theft removes millions of dollars from the American economy every year. We all pay for that loss through higher prices.

The federal Identity Theft and Assumption Deterrence Act, passed in 1998, made identity theft a federal crime. It carries maximum penalties of fifteen years in prison and substantial fines. That's all fine and good. Unfortunately, most people want law enforcement not to focus on white-collar crime but to clear the streets of murderers, rapists, drug dealers, violent criminals, and now terrorists. People want them rounded up because they pose a physical threat. I'm no fan of these guys either, but both you and I run a much higher risk of being victimized by an identity thief than by a mugger.

Police say they have little incentive to go out and arrest an identity thief. The cases are complex and require a lot of man-hours to crack. If they do arrest a thief, the local district attorney likely won't want to fool with the case because it's not high profile enough. The FBI is under a directive not to investigate any white-collar crime under $100,000 in value, due to lack of resources and the shift in manpower over to fighting terrorism. For a U.S. Attorney to prosecute a white-collar crime, the benchmark is $250,000. The identity thief knows that if he stays under that dollar amount, he's not likely to be prosecuted.

Even if you find an aggressive district attorney and he prosecutes a smaller case, you'd need to find a judge who would ultimately be willing to put that criminal in jail. In 1964 the U.S. prison system had a total of 68,000 inmates. That was at every level—federal, county, state, juvenile, women's, city. There were only 68,000 people behind bars in the entire United States. Today there are 2.1 million people behind bars. There are 4 million people on probation or parole somewhere in this country. Today, if a judge has four jail cells available to him and has a murderer, rapist, drug dealer, and three kidnappers, who's he going to send to jail? Not the identity thief.

I travel all over the world speaking, and I've found that in Europe, Australia, and Canada, companies are proactive. When they consider prevention techniques, they say, "We could do this, but then somebody might do that, so let's fix it so he can't do that." In the United States, however, people say, "We'll do this. If we have a problem, we'll fix it." As a society, Americans are much more reactive than proactive.

Remember, They Want You Too

Over my career trying to defeat fraud, I've developed a considerable amount of technology that's been implanted in credit cards, passports, driver's licenses, currencies, pharmaceuticals, airplane parts, and luxury items to prevent them from being counterfeited and altered. I've trained thousands of law enforcement agents—not only in this country but with Scotland Yard, the Royal Canadian Mounted Police, and the Australian Federal Police—in how to confront the problem of identity theft and fraud. And I think outside their box, as people like to say in the business world, because I long ago committed these crimes myself and am able to analyze them from a different perspective than other identity theft experts.

My primary goal in this book is to shine a light on the diabolically creative and clever criminal mind, so that you as a consumer can clearly understand just how vulnerable you are to somebody's becoming you. Even with the heightened discussions about security since the September 11 terrorist attacks, America boasts a citizenry far more trusting than that found in the rest of the world. Thieves thank us for that lackadaisical attitude, then take advantage of us.

Companies conduct business today by doling out credit like sugared party favors and do little if anything to ascertain that people really are who they say they are. But if companies are doing nothing about crime, then they're encouraging it, and that's where we are today: we're doing very little about crime. Instead, we keep passing the losses on to the American consumer.

Preventing identity theft is not simply a matter of following a checklist of ten or twenty steps. That unquestionably helps, and you'll come to my own suggestions later in this book. But to effectively keep this crime from happening to you, you need to understand how it works in a comprehensive way—what the telltale signs are, who does it, how thieves get information, and what they do with it.

Before I propose solutions, I'm going to take you through a detailed account of the inner workings of the crime. I'll explain how a washing machine warranty or the dog pound or even the good old Mormons can get you into trouble, and why you have to look out for Grandma and the zoology professor. Then I'll show you ways to prevent having your identity hijacked, including how to read those unreadable credit reports and privacy statements. I'll tell you why I've come to hate writing checks—once the most cherished form of paper in my life. I'll run through what you need to do if you are unfortunate enough to become a victim. Then I'll finish up with some thoughts on things you ought to lobby for with legislators and companies you regularly patronize to get their help in bringing this enormous problem under better control.

I have faith that we can make significant inroads into diminishing this ubiquitous crime, but it's not going to go away. If you haven't been a victim of identity theft, it's only because the thieves haven't gotten around to you yet. Everyone's somewhere on the list. Sooner or later, if things don't change, your turn will come.

2

The Next Victim—and It's You

A woman with especially fussy tastes had been searching for her dream house for what seemed like forever. Exasperated brokers were just about ready to give up on her. She looked at colonials, she looked at ranches, and she looked at split-levels, but everything always came up short. And then there it was: that postmodern house that was just the right size, in just the right neighborhood, and best of all, at just the right price. She had to move fast—others had appointments to view it that afternoon—and so she said she'd take it.

Both relieved and ecstatic, this woman was certain she had found the place that would make her happy for years to come. All that was left was to fill out the necessary paperwork, talk to the right people, and have the bank process her loan application. That didn't seem likely to be a problem, given her solid income and her long employment history with the same company. And she had always made a point of paying her bills promptly. Her friends even teased her about it. In other words, she simply had to do the paperwork and pick the moving-in date.

Then word came from the bank, and its verdict was bad. The mortgage was denied. Her credit was insufficient, and there was nothing they could do about it. She had never bought a house before and was not well versed in the calculus of mortgages. But still she was shocked. Downcast, the woman watched as another family moved into "her" dream home.

What went wrong?

Simple. For her, the deal-breaker was identity theft. While she had been minding her own business and paying her bills on time, an impersonator posing as her was making mincemeat out of her credit. Her doctor's receptionist had pilfered her information from his files, obtained multiple credit cards in her name, and then run them up to their limits, costing the woman the house she so fervently desired.

A sobering reality of modern-day life is that many identity theft victims have no idea that they've been victimized. Days, weeks, months, years, and even decades can go by while someone else spends money in your name without you knowing it. Often the signs are right there in front of you, but you don't recognize them for what they are. Being rejected for a mortgage certainly will get anyone's attention, but you'd be surprised by how many people assume that even this unanticipated jolt is somehow their fault, precipitated by a black mark on their record from years ago that they have forgotten about, or the result of their own miscalculation about their qualifications. They don't see it for what it actually is: the result of a criminal act.

The sooner you realize that you've been victimized, the sooner you can put a stop to the attack, and the better your chances are that the culprit might even be caught. Certain distinctive events are tip-offs, a sort of identity theft DNA that you should be alert to. My long familiarity with this crime has led me to conclude that there are four key events that suggest that someone has become a victim of identity theft.

1. Denied

Most people don't have any idea what the status of their credit is until the worst moment to find out: when they really need it. You apply for a loan, a mortgage, a job, or something else that typically requires a credit check. As far as you know, your credit is good, yet you're turned down. This, of course, is what happened to the hapless home-buyer. Denial of credit is the first sign of identity theft.

Another form of denial is a notification of a rate increase on your car insurance or home insurance, or word that your insurance is being canceled, when nothing adverse has changed in your life that would dictate that happening. There's always a reason, and it might well be identity theft.

When people are rejected for a mortgage or car loan, as I pointed out, they often do no real due diligence. They're humiliated and quickly presume it's their fault. Say you're turned down for a job. The company won't tell you the reason. You figure your résumé was weaker than you thought, or maybe you fumbled the interview or wore the wrong clothes. But actually a crook may well have wrecked your credit report. It happens all the time. Don't conclude it was just one more of life's bad blows and head to the nearest bar. If you're turned down for a job, forget the alcohol and the résumé-writing coach; get a copy of your credit report and look for the footprints of an identity thief.

Many times the sign that you've been victimized comes in a much subtler fashion. You get denied for a store credit card—

something you didn't really need anyway, and so you paid the incident no mind. Or you're refused an expansion of a personal line of credit. Don't presume you've simply hit your credit limit. A nineteen-year-old girl was repeatedly rejected for student loans and federal education grants during her four years of college. She shrugged it off, deciding she didn't satisfy the parameters. That wasn't the reason. An identity thief had applied for and received thirty-two credit cards under her name over five years and had racked up $150,000 in debt. So find out if the problem was caused by you or by someone who said they were you.

If you ask for a raise and get turned down, you might think it's because your boss is stingy or maybe your work performance isn't as good as you feel it is. But maybe your boss ran a credit check and discovered overdrawn accounts that weren't in fact yours. Assuming that you were a spendthrift, he may have decided not to give you more money to fritter away on indulgences.

The less established your credit is, the sooner this alarm will get tripped. If you're a new college graduate just beginning your career, you don't have much credit to begin with, so any drain created by an identity thief will quickly result in a denial. An application for cell phone service could do it.

Sometimes you're lucky and the denial is so absurd that something is obviously amiss. A fifteen-year-old in Georgia, eager to get his learner's permit and start driving, was turned down because state records indicated that he already had been issued a license. The records also showed that he was $5,000 in arrears on his child support payments. Not even in college, he was already in the hole.

But if you're making a decent income and have long-established good credit patterns, an identity thief could be spending money right alongside you for years, through numerous successful applications for additional credit, before you get surprised with a denial. That's why big-eyed identity thieves are picky and go after well-heeled victims. Even better is someone with solid credit who rarely applies for more. A favorite choice is an elderly person. Say she's in the nursing home with dementia, no longer sure who she is. She's never going to be looking for new credit.

Denial of credit is the most jarring way you're going to be tipped off that a thief has insinuated himself into your identity. But there are other ways as well.

2. Ripped Off

Out of the blue and much to her distress, a Virginia woman found out that more than $200,000 in loans had been taken out in her name in New Jersey. Huh? She had visited that state exactly once in her life. How did it happen? A man in Virginia who worked at a mortgage company where she had once taken out a loan managed to get hold of her Social Security number and used it to secure two car loans, two personal loans, and a mortgage. The woman had no idea any of this mischief had happened until he began missing the payments and she was asked to make them.

That experience was eye-opening all right. But how about the unfortunate California woman who was notified by the IRS that she owed roughly $1 million in back taxes? She had good reason to be in shock about this staggering bill, since she hadn't even worked in five years, having taken up motherhood after giving birth to a child. For years a number of illegal immigrants had been working under her Social Security number while declining to bother with that nasty business known as tax-paying.

It's a pretty good tip-off that something is wrong when your credit card, bank, or other financial statement contains charges that you never made. An even more obvious tip-off is a statement for a credit card or loan, or from the tax authorities, that you didn't know you had.

On a credit card bill, you should immediately inquire about any suspicious charge, even one for $2.50. It could be the beginning of a raging nightmare. And don't be easily put off. Suppose something looks suspicious, you call the credit card company—I've done it—and they don't know what that charge is. They give you the phone number of the vendor in question. You call it and get one of those automated menus—press this for that, press that for this—and you never reach a live person. Meanwhile it's a toll charge, so you hang up and accomplish nothing. Don't let it go—dispute it.

If a merchant calls to verify a charge that you never made, don't just say that's wrong and assume the merchant will delete it. He might delete it without doing anything beyond that. Assume the worst—that it's part of a larger identity theft against you.

If you see something fishy on a bank or brokerage statement, go to the bank or broker and find out if it's a mistake or something sinister.

Security officials at large department stores tell me that the biggest problem they face isn't shoplifting or fraudulent checks—it's these instant store credit cards. Suppose you're shopping, and a salesperson asks, "Do you have one of our cards? It'll just take thirty seconds to get one." She asks for your name, where you work, your date of birth, and your Social Security number, then she checks your credit, it's great, and presto, you've got a temporary card with a $2,000 limit. If you're an identity thief, you didn't give your name, you gave someone else's name. In twenty minutes you buy $2,000 worth of merchandise with it, and thirty days later the bill goes to somebody who had never set foot in the store.

Don't conclude it's a mix-up—follow up.

3. Harassed and Hounded

It's the most dreaded phone call, the one that arrives first thing in the morning, before you've even had coffee or a shower. Or it comes at dinner, instantly spoiling your appetite. The obnoxious guy from the collection agency. It's bad enough when you actually owe someone money, but when you get calls to collect on debts that you never incurred, an alarm ought to go off in your head.

The attitude of a lot of consumers is not to respond to calls from debt collectors. They think that their payment just hasn't caught up with the bill, or they're sure they're not in arrears, and so they tell the guy on the phone, "Well, you know what, buddy? You can go to hell. I never bought that. I'll catch you later." And then they slam down the phone.

Well, that's exactly what the guy is expecting you to say. That's what everyone says when a debt collector calls.

Even if that debt collector believes you, he has no ability or authority to look into whether you are in fact the person who incurred the debt. You need to go to the source. It's a much wiser consumer who takes fifteen minutes and asks the collection guy, "Okay, can you give me the name of the company that says I owe them? Because I need to call them up and get this straight." Get the information in writing from the collector, then contact the company.

When you speak to the company, tell them that you didn't purchase anything from them or apply for a loan, and if they'd like a sworn affidavit, tell them you'll send it. If it's a debt with the fence company, call the fence company. If it's a debt with the venetian blind maker in Laramie, call the blind maker in Laramie.

Sometimes the hounding call isn't from a person—it's one of those prerecorded announcements telling you to call a toll-free number. These calls are the easiest of all to blow off, and people usually do. You shouldn't.

4. Where Did the Mail Go?

A while ago police in Port Orchard, Washington, came across a suspicious-looking pickup truck parked alongside a road. When they took a look inside, they found it crammed with stolen mail— hundreds of letters, a raft of gas bills and bank statements, some greeting cards, and plenty of junk mail. The occupants of the truck were almost incoherent, because they were high on methamphetamine. They were on their way to a mobile home, where they regularly traded stolen mail to identity thieves in exchange for hits of meth. The thieves sorted out the useless letters and used the ones that contained personal information to assume identities.

At first you might even be grateful that the flow of junk mail has slacked off and you haven't seen a bill in two months. But if your bills stop coming, or there's an unusual decline in the quantity of mail you receive, that's a problem well worth investigating. It might mean that an identity thief has stolen your mail or has changed the address on your credit card statement so you won't notice the fraudulent charges on your account. And guess what? The thief isn't taking care of those bills for you. He might be making the minimum payments to keep the credit card issuer from contacting you, but that's a small price to pay for how much he's charging to you.

My kids use a MasterCard, for which the bill always comes

about the sixteenth of the month. One time after that date had passed, I asked my wife what the kids' spending had been like. She said, "You know, I haven't seen the bill." I told her that if it didn't come in a few days, call the credit card company. It did arrive, and it was nothing, but you need to be alert to changes in the rhythm. Credit card companies send out bills like clockwork, so if yours doesn't arrive when it should, there's a good chance something is amiss.

Call them up, and they might tell you they sent their statements out late this month. Or they might say it went out a week ago. Then ask them to fax over the statement. Check and see if it's accurate.

Because of complaints about unauthorized changes of address, the post office has begun sending out verifications to both the old and the new addresses. Does this help? Yes. Is it enough? No. A smart crook will know about this precautionary procedure, and so after he's finished with the change of address, he'll steal the verification that comes to your home. What the post office ought to do is be more vigilant about confirming that it's you when you come in to fill out the change-of-address card.

Don't think that a missing bill or financial account statement is the sole tip-off. Identity theft could involve the most innocuous of mail. A doctor in Rochester, Minnesota, found out that she was a victim when she called to inquire why her *New England Journal of Medicine* hadn't come. Funny thing, it was being forwarded, along with her other mail, to a ring of Nigerians in Brooklyn. And you can bet they weren't medical students.

The Final Sign: No Sign

Often there is no sign at all that you've become the target of identity theft. Identity theft is frequently a stealth crime. Crafty criminals have become extremely adept at covering their tracks, and they keep getting better at it. I know victims who were impersonated for more than a decade before they caught on. The point I'm trying to make is, don't think that if none of these four alarms go off, you're safe. Complacency always works to the very profitable benefit of criminals.

But how does the cycle start? Where does a thief get the necessary ingredients that allow him to step into your identity and rob you of it?

3

The Road to Becoming You

The story about the stray dog really put things over the top for me. Someone I know had spotted a dog wandering aimlessly around a park near her home. It bore no collar or identifying tag, but it certainly seemed friendly enough. With minimal effort, she managed to corral it and prod it into her car, then drove it over to the dog pound. The person on duty accepted the animal, thanked her perfunctorily, and said that if she didn't mind, he needed to get a little information. He began rattling off questions from a list: name, address, Social Security number, on and on.

"Wait a minute," she said, a little taken aback. "Why do you need all this information about me? It's not my dog. I found this dog."

The dog pound guy said, "Well, it's on my form."

"Look," she said, "I'm not giving you my Social Security number. If you won't accept the dog without it, I'll just take it back to the park."

The guy finally relented. But most people unthinkingly disclose this information, not because it makes any sense to disclose it but simply because someone asked for it. That person doesn't even know why it's needed. It's just "on my form." Then a thief or some worker at the pound gets hold of it and either sells it or uses it himself to take over your identity.

If your reward for being a Good Samaritan and shepherding a lost dog to the pound is that you put yourself at risk for identity theft, then the world is even crazier than I thought.

Remember That Washer

The truth is, you don't have to tattoo your Social Security number on your forehead or lend your credit card to random strangers to become a victim of identity theft. When I was a teenager, only three people knew my Social Security number—me, the government, and my employer. Alas, in this age of information overload and fast-moving technology, Social Security numbers are everywhere. Everyone seems to need it—the grocer, the video store, the school, the health club, the electric company, the candlestick maker, and the dog pound. I rented a storage locker for one of my sons, something tens of thousands of people do all the time, and they wanted my date of birth, driver's license, and Social Security number. Why? One reason: it was on the form. People don't realize that in almost all cases, they don't have to answer these questions, but they do so anyway.

Such generosity affords criminals limitless opportunities to obtain the information necessary to commit identity theft, often in a matter of minutes. On days when I'm feeling particularly frustrated about this kind of crime, I say to myself, "Crooks don't even have to try. Information is thrown right in their laps." I might not feel as disturbed about it if criminals at least worked hard for their ill-gotten gains.

Everywhere you look there are all kinds of resources open to the public. Phone books and directories, voter registration lists, county assessor records, questionnaires, warranty cards, motor vehicle reports, police reports, license and deed transfers, military records, bankruptcy filings, Social Security Administration death files, marriage records, divorce records, state professional licenses, boat registrations—all of these records are public. Lots of people get entreaties in the mail to refinance their mortgage at a lower rate. The invitations mention how large your loan is and who holds it. How do they know? Public records.

To root into people's lives, I don't even have to get into the car and go anywhere. I just go online. It's that simple.

The Internet is one of the most versatile research tools a criminal has ever been handed. It's no exaggeration to say that there are thousands of free and paid resources on the Web that can be unsuspectingly used for identity theft. An avalanche of personal information that is compiled by private companies gets housed and traded in the multibillion-dollar information industry. This information hasn't been stolen or even been coerced out of you. You willingly provided it.

Let's say you apply for a new credit card, and you don't bother to check that box that says you don't want your information shared. You can bet it will be shared. You enter a sweepstakes to win a one-week trip to Cancún. Everything you write on that entry will be sold.

Every time you share a piece of information about yourself, without obtaining a binding guarantee that it will not be sold or shared, that information instantly enters the public domain and becomes fodder for that expanding information industry. The only exception is medical information. For that to be shared, a release has to be signed. Unfortunately, these days it's your credit health, not your medical health, that interests criminals. As these dossiers build up, they become permanent. You have no way of knowing what's in them, and no way of suppressing them or deleting any of the information. Identity thieves can buy a CD-ROM containing birth and death records, and they can apply for a new birth certificate by mail—not just your birth certificate, anyone's birth certificate. There are websites that sell Social Security numbers for under $50. It's very disturbing—unless you happen to be a criminal.

Have you ever really looked at the questionnaire you get when, say, you buy a washing machine? Did you fill it out? Why? For what purpose? Did you ever truly read it? It starts out pretty simple, asking what influenced you to buy the product, what type of unit you bought, and whether you've owned this brand before.

But by the time you get to question number nineteen or so, they are asking for the date of your birth, the dates of your children's births, your marital status, whether you own or rent your house, your income range, your level of education, your profession, what credit cards you have, and what you read. By the time you've finished, you've given away your profile.

Why does a washing machine vendor need all this information? Why would you fill it out? You have to understand, the company doesn't need it but will sell it to data-gatherers like ChoicePoint and LexisNexis. The biggest customers are insurance companies. Let's say an insurance company is thinking about insuring me for $1 million, so it asks about me at one of the major information providers, which tells it, "Well, I don't know if you want to insure him." "Why not?" "Well, he's big into skydiving." "How do you know that?" "Well, he reads all these skydiving magazines."

I may have blown that insurance policy when I bought the washing machine, but that's the least of my worries. This information about me is now in play, being sold and resold, and who knows whose hands it is getting into? Identity theft is about stealing a little here, a little there, and before you know it, the thief is you. With very little effort, he has more than enough source material to become you.

Thanks a Lot, Mormons

Information about you is everywhere. I know it, and you ought to know it. Rather than wonder whether that's true, go online.

Visit the website familysearch.org. In fact, I would implore you to pull it up on your browser. Let me tell you a couple of things about it. First of all, it's the third-largest database in the world, and it's owned and operated by the Church of Jesus Christ of Latter-Day Saints, also known as the Mormons, in Salt Lake City. When you go to their home page, you'll see some buttons that enable you to search family history. One allows you to access death records. Just click that button, and up on the screen will come a template for you to type a name and address. Think of the name of someone you know who has died in the last couple of months—or in the last two hundred years.

I typed in the name of my late father, Frank William Abagnale, Sr. I pressed Enter. Within thirty seconds, up came my father's date of birth, date of death, and Social Security number, as well as the last five cities he lived in prior to his death. Because I had searched for Abagnale, I was able to scroll down to more than two hundred Abagnales—aunts, uncles, cousins who had passed away. Some cousins I didn't know—third cousins probably. Some died when they were twenty-one and twenty-eight. They must have been killed in Vietnam or in car accidents. But for each person, I had the dates of birth and death, a Social Security number, and the last five localities where they lived. Everything available was derived from publicly available sources.

Identity thieves love to pick up old newspapers and scour the obituaries, not as you and I do, to see if there's someone we know, but to look for someone they'd like to become. They'll read, "Robert L. Carter, president and chief executive of a multimillion-dollar corporation and founder of dot-com company XYZ, died yesterday on Interstate 71 while traveling eastbound"—blah, blah, blah—"survived by his wife and family." A few months later they pull up the name on familysearch.org and retrieve his Social Security number. They apply for a credit card in his name. No credit card bureau in the world, let alone the United States, keeps track of deaths. So they get the credit card. Carter's widow gets the bill.

If I want your Social Security number, all I need is your name. I can go to the biggest online provider of Social Security numbers, DocuSearch.com. For more than a dozen years they've been selling Social Security numbers. That's their business: forty-nine bucks. All I do is enter your name and address and pay the $49, and they give me your Social Security number. They insist they sell only to people who satisfy certain criteria, but that's not a deterrent for imaginative crooks. What they're doing, of course, is perfectly legal. There are no laws in the United States—federal, state, county, or city—that prohibit the sale of Social Security numbers.

If you go on this website and you have a child who's maybe nine years old, he's got a Social Security number assigned to him that he hasn't even used yet. Type in his name and address, and you'll get his Social Security number.

While you've surfing the Web, try NetDetective.com or just NetDetective2000, and you'll be routed to a company whose ad says it all: "We'll tell you everything and anything about anybody"—for a fee. The fee is $150. What they'll tell you is where you work, what your salary is, your date of birth, your Social Security number, who you're married to, and who you've been married to. They'll tell you whether you've had a DWI or DUI, if you've ever been arrested, where you went to elementary school, where you went to high school, and where you went to college—you name it.

They claim that they do cheap background checks for $150. So if I were an identity thief, why would I go out and waste my time looking up this information when, for $150, I have it at my fingertips? What's $150? I'm going to get a credit card in your name, probably with a $5,000 limit, so the $150 is simply the cost of doing business.

Other sites, like DocuSearch.com, will furnish personal but public information for anywhere from $49 to $150. You can even pick up what the FBI knows about you.

The disseminators of all this information, especially the ones that do it for free, defend what they are doing. In fact, they're proud of it. They think of it as the democratization of information. If some people have access to your information, they reason, why shouldn't everyone? Well, everyone includes identity thieves.

Look Out for the Satellites

Which brings me to ZabaSearch.com. It's a doozy of a website. This service is largely free, and it ought to be, since *zaba* is derived from the Greek word *tzaba*, which means "free." Type in somebody's name, and you can get all their addresses for the last decade, their phone numbers (even if they're unlisted), date of birth, and more. If you're willing to part with $20, and many criminals won't need to because they've already got enough information, you can get a more detailed background report on someone.

All this is the least scary aspect of the site. The most astonishing thing about ZabaSearch is that up until recently it allowed you to actually see somebody's home, courtesy of overhead satellite cameras. I'm talking about homes of movie stars, of politicians, of chief executives, of your mother, of you.

You could've gone to the site at any hour of the day or night and plugged in an address. It could've been in Connecticut or North Dakota, it didn't matter. Within moments the screen would fill with aerial footage of that house, shot by satellite cameras.

It would transmit live photos (and other sites are still experimenting with them), and so if little Sally was out riding her bike, you'd see her in her pigtails. If Dad was mowing the lawn, you'd see him in his cargo shorts pushing the mower. And if no one was home, you'd see that too. As far as criminals are concerned, I think you get the idea. Thieves could study the pictures and notice that Dad left for work at seven-thirty, Mom took the kids to school at eight-fifteen, there was no sign of any maid, so let's move in. They'd get a sense of whether it was a ritzy house worth invading, if there was a burglar alarm warning. The old days of donning dark glasses and staking out a house in a black sedan parked down the street are long gone.

When robbers rifle through the contents of a house today, they're often far less interested in the wall safe and the wife's diamond earrings than in names, account numbers, and Social Security numbers, troves that can reap them much larger rewards. Information—strings of black digits on sheets of paper—has become the central fulcrum of crime in America.

One day I went ahead and called up my own house on ZabaSearch. Amazingly, I was able to move the image and see six houses down one way and six houses up another way.

Now this can't be legal, can it? I'm afraid it is. And the reason is the usual one. All of the information, including those photographs of your home, comes from publicly available sources, government records, and commercial sources.

Zaba got enough heat for the satellite photos that the last time I looked they had stopped showing them and instead had substituted maps that locate a person's home. But you can still go to Google Earth and get satellite images. Someone I know called up his own apartment building in Nevada, and the photo was so clear that he could identify specific cars in the parking lot. What worries me is that other sites will get deeper into this kind of thing, especially freewheeling foreign-based sites.

You can even go online and buy someone's phone records—cell phone or land line—and that's legal, because the data brokers that sell the information are basically unregulated. In fact, the Chicago police department had to warn its own officers to beware that their records might be up for sale at dozens of sites. How do brokers get the call records? They claim they get them legally, such as by finding them in the garbage. Yeah, right. In fact, they do it the way a lot of information is illicitly obtained, by the social engineering trick known as *pretexting*. Once they know a cell phone number and Social Security number, they can call up the phone company and pretend to be the subscriber in need of his records.

So much information already circulates about people's personal lives, but it can quickly get a lot worse. These digital dossiers could potentially include things like patterns of Internet use, what sites people go to, and what they do on them. The number of security cameras is proliferating. There's been lots of joking advice that you need to make sure you look your best when you go out to run your errands, because you're liable to be videotaped a dozen or more times. Well, it's possible to connect those cameras to websites that can add the footage to these dossiers.

Even the Government Does Its Part

We expect the government to look out for us. They're awfully busy, but after all, it is what we pay them to do. Yet they go and do their part to give identity thieves a helping hand.

I have three sons. By federal law, all eighteen-year-old boys must register with the Selective Service Administration in case the government brings back the draft. A postcard is sent out to the boy. It is addressed on one side to the government and the postage is paid. The boy fills out the other side and then drops the postcard in the mail. It asks for date of birth, Social Security number, and full and current address. Down in the bottom right-hand corner he writes his signature in a box so that it can be scanned and put on file.

Once he drops that card in the mail, how many hundreds of people are going to see it? Certainly plenty of low-level postal employees have been known to sell these numbers to criminal rings. Lots of Selective Service workers either see them lying around or are involved in processing them. What if the card tumbles out of the mail carrier's bag and is lying on the street? Do you care who happens to pick it up? I do.

When my sons filled the postcards out, I put them in check envelopes so no one could see through them, and then I self-addressed them and stuck on my own thirty-seven-cent stamps and mailed them. It involved a little more effort and a slight expense. But I was minimizing my sons' risk.

There is no better victim than an eighteen-year-old on his way to college. He has no credit, and for the next four years he's not likely to get it, so for the next four years a thief can become him with minimal interference.

What about our soldiers? There's been a lot of pressure on the government to get them better body armor to protect their lives, but what about also protecting their private information? The Social Security number is used everywhere in the military: on IDs, sometimes to log in to base computers, to sign in to meetings, on official communications. Soldiers have even been told to stencil their Social Security numbers right onto their duffel bags, which they openly lug through airports, blatantly advertising their identity to the world. The Defense Department has begun to control things a little better of late, but there's still much work to be done.

I looked up what enlistees in the National Guard are told to bring to boot camp. It's not only three sets of underwear (white), dental floss, and a hairbrush or six-inch black comb; they're told to bring their Social Security card, driver's license, a direct deposit form from their checking account signed by a bank official, a copy of their marriage certificate or divorce decree (if applicable), a certified copy of their birth certificate, their college transcript or high school diploma, their spouse's Social Security number if a member of the military, and birth certificates for children under eighteen. They're told not to bring more than fifty dollars in cash, I guess because of worries about theft. Worries about theft? All of that documentation is an all-in-one identity theft gift package.

So even our own government is making simple mistakes that put people in jeopardy of having their identities lifted.

Come On In, the Surf's Great

Californians go body surfing. Identity thieves go shoulder surfing. Let's tag along and watch.

A thief trolling for information will venture out to a part of town, say a gated community, where the homes are worth $1 million to $2 million. He'll then look for a busy supermarket nearby. He'll park right next to the store's sliding doors and sit in his car with his eyes open. He's looking for the Mercedes, the Range Rover, the Jaguar. He's looking at watches, clothing, jewelry. When he finds the right person walking in, he gets out and walks in right behind her. She buys groceries; he buys groceries. She goes to the checkout; he goes to the checkout. But at some point she's going to take out her checkbook and place it on that little ledge beside the conveyor belt and write a check. And when she does, he'll be standing right next to her.

It takes a thief about eight seconds to memorize the face of a check, so even before she's dated it, he's finished. He has trained himself to focus on the last name in the upper left-hand corner, and only the last name (he'll worry about the first name later), as well as the city. He'll pick up on the bank's logo but never the bank's name or the street, city, or state that it's in. He ignores the long routing and transit number, the nine digits in the bracket, and picks up only on the account number at the end of the bracket. And he glances at the check number.

He goes outside and jots the information down on a piece of paper. He pulls out the check reorder coupon from *Parade* magazine and fills it out. Name and address he'd like on the check? He goes to the white pages and looks for that last name. Let's say it's Worthington. There it is, something like Sally W. Worthington, 127 East Locust Avenue, Lexington, Kentucky. He writes it in. Name of your bank? He saw the U.S. Bank logo, so U.S. Bank. He turns to the American Bankers Association key routing directory on the Internet and looks up U.S. Bank's key, and there's the routing and transit number. He memorized the account number. He assumes that a bank as sophisticated as U.S. Bank is probably tracking check numbers by some sort of artificial intelligence program, so if the shopper was on 1056, he's going to start with something like 1065. Style of check? Well, you have flags on your checks, so he's going to order checks with flags. How many? Two hundred. Last question: if you'd like these checks sent to an address other than the address printed on the face of the checks, say so here. He writes down his P.O. box number.

Ten days later he's got two hundred of the woman's checks. He can spend them and cash them as if he were she. If the woman has money in her account, he's going to get it. If she doesn't have money, no problem, she probably has overdraft protection, so he's going to get it anyway.

It's a nifty little trick for the well-trained thief. One of the nice things that has happened to criminals in recent years is that all those crooks with bum memories who could never quite master shoulder surfing can now play the game too. They just stand next to you at the checkout line on their cell phone, snapping pictures of your check while you're writing it. When they get back home, they download the photos onto the computer screen, and they're in business.

The Doctor, the Department Store, the College

Just by going through your workaday routines, living your life the way you always have, you're spreading your information like grass seed all over the place.

Begin with your visit to the doctor. As a new patient, the receptionist asks you to complete a form that asks for your name, address, and phone number, as well as your employer's name, address, and phone number, along with your health history. The most important thing the doctor needs, the health history, is the one thing the identity thief can do without. The receptionist asks to see your health insurance card. She doesn't just look at it and hand it back. She copies it. She requests your driver's license and copies that too. Your copay is paid with a check drawn on your bank account. You may not realize it, but you have just provided enough information for someone to become you. Then she sticks all those copies in your medical record. In many doctors' offices the staff keeps rack files that aren't locked up or secured in any way, just begging to be stolen.

You drop in at the department store. Someone approaches you and says he's security and asks for help in catching a deviant employee. Could you fill out a credit application? You do. The guy reviews it, says it looks fine, and asks you to give it to the designated employee. Guess what? The guy's the problem. He's not security, and now he's got your information.

Or a thief wanders around a department store looking for a customer about to make a purchase. Using his cell phone, he calls the cashier and says he's store security checking up on the customer and asks her for the person's account information.

All parents want their child to get a solid college education, and in these competitive days you need to apply to a raft of colleges to make sure you get into a good one. It's hard work but is made easier by online applications. For the identity thief, however, this is a rewarding trend. When you apply to college, the schools want your Social Security number. In fact, it often becomes the application identification number. For all related documentation—teacher evaluations, personal recommendations, and supplemental material like tapes of you playing the oboe or setting a state record in the pole vault—the college tells you to put your Social Security number on it so that it will find its way to the appropriate file. Meanwhile, if your parents apply for financial aid, they have to send along an application including a wealth of financial information and tax forms containing their Social Security numbers and address. Kids frequently apply to ten or twelve colleges apiece. Tons of people at those colleges have access to that material. The information is practically waving in the faces of crooks.

Some companies, government agencies, and even colleges have been known to ask participants to put their name and Social Security number on a sign-in roster for seminars and meetings. Doesn't seem like a big deal, does it? Well, guess what? Identity thieves make a point of deliberately signing up toward the end of a page so that they can jot down all that juicy information on the lines above.

The FBI has been warning people for some time about the jury duty scam. Crooks posing as U.S. court employees call people and tell them they've been selected for jury duty—and that they need to verify their names and Social Security numbers. If they refuse, they're threatened with fines. As it happens, the court system actually uses the good old-fashioned mail to enlist citizens in jury service. Representatives never call prospective jurors or ask for personal information over the phone.

Let's not forget the lowly pickpocket. Once upon a time these sticky-fingered criminals stole your wallet for the money inside. If only we could dial back the clock to those good old days. Nowadays they want data—a Social Security card, a PIN number scribbled on a scrap of paper, a driver's license, a health insurance card, a company ID card with a Social Security number. Pretty much the only safe thing to carry in your wallet today is actual cash.

I Thought They Locked Mailboxes

One of the great repositories of criminal source material stands openly on street corners and in front of houses in every community in the country: the mailbox.

You probably don't realize this, but mailboxes frequently aren't locked, or if they are, it doesn't take a bodybuilder to get them open. So anyone wandering down the street can open one up and help himself to as much mail as he likes. In fact, he can even put up his own fake mailbox and collect mail that way. Thieves don't want the latest issue of *Cosmopolitan* or *Motor Trend,* and love letters aren't of much interest, but boy do they adore preapproved credit card invitations, electric bills, bank statements, brokerage accounts, and maybe even a fresh order of checks. Yes, the mail has it all for the budding identity thief. The credit card overtures alone will keep him busy for months. Americans get bombarded with something on the order of eight offers a month per household.

Thieves will pluck the mail right out of your own mailbox. A twenty-two-year-old woman and her sixteen-year-old friend were caught in Hawaii opening mailboxes in subdivisions. As a cover, they stuffed leaflets promoting a babysitting service inside the boxes as they were extracting the mail.

A Pennsylvania man had applied for a loan from his local bank, then changed his mind and went with an alternative institution. He asked his bank to return the personal information he had supplied them. They mailed it back, and he was shocked to find that the envelope had been opened. Some of the papers were missing, and others were ripped. Unfortunately, you're not always the first person to open your mail.

Law enforcement reports a tremendous increase in identity theft among meth addicts, known as "tweakers" or "cranksters," because it's easy money and they're well suited to staying up all day and night rooting through mailboxes. In Georgia a band of twenty thieves dubbed the Mailbox Meth Gang cruised subdivisions for mail containing checks and bank statements. Thieves appreciate housing developments that bunch the mailboxes together in a stand-alone structure. A crowbar rips the entire face off of the structure, and the thieves help themselves to the mail. When they were caught, the Mailbox Meth Gang had a laptop with fourteen thousand credit card numbers stored in it. In Arizona, a hotbed of identity theft, the connection between identity theft and mailbox-raiding meth addicts is so great that the attorney general routinely sends an investigator with identity theft experience along on meth lab busts.

Keep in mind that January is identity thieves' favorite month— and they never take any vacation time then. That's when the mail is stuffed with tax documents from employers, banks, brokerage houses, and the government. Crooks eagerly look forward to this deluge all year.

As long as an identity thief is wearing his old clothes, he can always go Dumpster diving. Remember all those credit card offers? Most of them end up in the trash. So do a lot of other juicy documents—often unopened bank statements and already-paid bills. During times when the stock market is tanking, many people don't even open their 401(k) statements and brokerage reports, sometimes just chucking them into the garbage. That's okay. Identity thieves don't mind opening them.

A woman went to a post office and watched as people getting

their mail from post office boxes threw out merchandise catalogs that didn't interest them. When they left, she dug them out of the garbage, since they often contained names and account numbers. Then she ordered merchandise under their identities.

One of the nice things about Dumpster diving for crooks—the ones that don't mind getting spaghetti sauce on their hands and competing with rats—is that while opening a mailbox can get nasty if the police happen to notice, Dumpster diving is perfectly legal. As long as you don't venture onto private property, there's no law against rooting through somebody's garbage. In fact, the Supreme Court, in a 1988 ruling, confirmed this fact.

California v. Greenwood, decided in May 1988, not only buttressed the powers of law enforcement, it also provided welcome solace to identity thieves. Police had suspected that Billy Greenwood was dealing drugs from his house. Since they didn't have sufficient evidence to secure a warrant to search the premises, they sifted through the garbage bags stacked on the curb. They found enough incriminating evidence to get their warrant and convict Greenwood. Greenwood's lawyers, however, contended that the garbage search violated the Fourth Amendment's search and seizure guarantee. The six-to-two court ruling held that trash at the curbside is not protected by the Constitution. The majority opinion argued that there exists no reasonable expectation of privacy for trash on public streets "readily accessible to animals, children, scavengers, snoops, and other members of the public." They might have added identity thieves.

I Just Wanted to Figure Out the Microwave

You're probably well aware that much customer service these days is outsourced, and I mean really outsourced. It used to be that when you called a help line in New York, someone picked up the phone in Omaha. Now they pick up the phone in New Delhi or Singapore or maybe at the Arctic Circle. That may make economic sense, and when you're trying to figure out how to turn on your satellite dish, it may not matter a great deal. But it can cause you problems.

Today companies in the business of quality assurance contract with businesses to eavesdrop on customer calls made in this country to make sure that consumers are treated politely and in a helpful manner. To check up on those inquiries, they'll also read e-mail exchanges. Now, it's true that many companies regularly listen in on a percentage of customer calls for quality assurance purposes, and you're often alerted with an automatic message that your call might be monitored. You probably assume that that means some sort of supervisor will do the monitoring.

These quality assurance companies, however, have people listening in on call-center calls who are—guess where—in India. And these are calls during which Social Security numbers and credit card numbers, among other personal information, may be shared. Dishonest workers can be an issue anywhere, but this situation ups the ante because American privacy laws don't have jurisdiction abroad. If a crooked infiltrator works at one of these places, he's getting information that he can use or can sell to criminal rings, and to top it off, he's actually getting paid to do it. American authorities can't touch him.

The companies in the business of quality assurance say that they have exacting confidentiality standards, that all workers sign nondisclosure agreements that bar them from sharing the information outside the company. But a crook is a crook, and a piece of paper with his signature on it rarely inhibits him. I don't know about you, but the thought that I might be speaking to someone at the department store down the block, while a very low-paid worker in another country thousands of miles away is furiously taking notes, doesn't give me great comfort.

Shouldn't we know more about the hiring and screening practices of these companies? Shouldn't a consumer be notified that his phone conversations or e-mails about his clogged trash compactor might be overheard or read by someone in India, so that he can be cautious about divulging any sensitive information that could be exploited?

Let's Go Phishing

Like most people these days, I get an awful lot of e-mail—two hundred or so messages a day. It's the usual mix of business communications, personal exchanges, and utter nonsense. I thought I'd share a few recent arrivals. You'll probably find them familiar.

One contained the great news that "as a result of our recent lottery draws" my ticket number won in the second category and that I was due a lump-sum payout of $1 million. To validate the notice, the promotion in question was said to be sponsored by the likes of the Sultan of Brunei and Bill Gates as a way to encourage use of the Internet. Amazingly, I had never bought a ticket, and $1 million was simply second prize. A pretty reliable rule of thumb is that you don't win lotteries that you don't enter. Still, all I had to do was fill out nine simple lines of information, including name, age, and Social Security number, and then say how I wanted to get the money—by check, wire transfer, or cash. Oh, how I wished it were true, if for no other reason than to see what it feels like to get a package in the mail stuffed with $1 million in cash.

Another e-mail was from Olu Ade, identified as the personal accountant to Engr. Arthur B. Luttrell, a foreign national who used to work with Shell Development Company in Nigeria. Bad news, it seemed, had visited Mr. Luttrell. He had been in a nasty car accident along with his wife and three children, and "all occupants of the vehicle unfortunately lost their lives." After an exhaustive search for relatives proved futile, Mr. Ade had somehow settled on me as the fitting heir. He needed an "emergency response" before the proceeds were confiscated by the bank. Half of the estate was going to Mr. Ade and for expenses, but since the total was $11.5 million, one could hardly argue that my split of $5.75 million from a complete stranger was stingy. Again, all I had to do was fill in the blanks and wait for the bounty.

Still another e-mail purportedly came from the wife of a Lebanese businessman who had been killed in an explosion in Beirut. He left behind $86 million, and $20 million of it was mine if I helped get the money into the United States. The next day I heard from an eighteen-year-old girl from Ghana, whose father, a wealthy cocoa merchant, "was poisoned to death by his business associates on one of their outings." If I agreed to be a foster parent, I would merit a 20 percent cut of his $8.2 million estate.

These are all versions of a classic scam, with very long legs. The traps are known as Nigerian Letter scams or 419 letters, named after the pertinent African criminal code under which they can be prosecuted.

In the fairly recent past these straightforward cons were designed to get your bank information so that the crooks could raid your account. They had no further interest in you. But as identity theft has become the top game in town, these scams have been reconfigured to steal your identity information. They don't necessarily even ask for your bank account number anymore. They'd rather get your name and Social Security number and use them for a full-scale identity assumption.

These e-mails, and numerous other renditions, are called phishing attacks. We've all been fishing. But phishing is a much bigger recreational sport for identity thieves. And today it's one of the most productive ways they gather their source material.

This crime started fairly innocently in the mid-1990s, when America Online was charging its users by the hour. Chatty teenagers looking to figure out a way around their bulging bills began sending out randomly directed e-mails under the guise of being AOL customer service agents, hunting for account IDs and passwords. They used the ones that came back to remain online on someone else's dime. The kids referred to this practice as *phishing*, derived from *fishing*, the deliberate misspelling being a bow to the "phone phreaks" of yesteryear who got their kicks stealing long-distance phone service from Ma Bell.

Once AOL and other service providers switched to flat monthly pricing, this sort of phishing was no longer necessary. By then, however, professional phishermen had entered the sport and claimed it as their own.

Phishing is highly efficient. Sending spam e-mail out to a million people doesn't cost a cent. Every phish that is hooked is worth thousands or tens of thousands or hundreds of thousands of dollars.

The standard strategy is to phish using a cover that people are likely to recognize and trust, usually a well-known and reputable bank, brokerage house, corporation, or government agency. Citibank, eBay, and AOL have been common choices. The message will set forth a phony but believable reason why you need to respond with your personal information. Generally speaking, phishing uses two broad categories of bait: that which relies on greed and that which relies on fear.

The greed approaches typically inform victims that they are getting something for nothing—one of the biggest fraud flags going. A new service is being rolled out at a financial institution, you are told, and lucky you have been chosen to get the service free for a limited period. Other times you're asked to fill out a bank survey in exchange for a modest monetary reward. Then there are the travel incentives: give us your information, and you'll get a discount on a flight or a resort hotel stay. Many common ruses tell you that you've won an iPod or another prize of some sort. One e-mail simply reported that someone had sent you $450, who knows why, and all you had to do was sign up for an account to receive it.

More often than not, however, the bait of choice used by phishermen is fear. Something may be amiss with your bank account— can we verify your information? Or there's been a computer glitch, and your account information has been lost. Or—the one I like—we think your account information has been stolen, and we have to freeze your account immediately until we get your private information to get it functioning again. Here are thieves, out to steal your account, telling you they're going to protect you from themselves.

Or—horrors—your credit card has been charged for buying some child pornography. Did you buy such porn? No? Well, give us your credit information pronto, and we'll remove this stain from your record. One actual e-mail notified its victims that their bank account had been charged $287.64 to Adultfriend Finder for a one-year subscription. If you're married, you certainly don't want that on your bill.

Here's a recent hoax e-mail that purports to come from the FBI:

Dear Sir/Madam,

We have logged your IP-address on more than 30 illegal Web-sites. Important: Please answer our questions! The list of questions are attached.

Yours faithfully,

Steven Allison

Federal Bureau of Investigation—FBI

Some phishing attacks, said to be from the IRS, tell of a tax investigation. Others claim to be from the Federal Deposit Insurance Corporation, the entity that insures bank accounts, saying that your federal deposit insurance has been canceled because of alleged fraud. It asks that you click on a link and fill in your personal information so things can be straightened out.

Many identity thieves opt for the fear route, because when people get agitated, they quickly abandon common sense and do foolhardy things—like pretty much whatever they're asked to do.

If you fall for the pitch, and countless people do, you're asked either to respond to the e-mail or, more commonly, to click on a linked Web address and answer the questions there. So many of these notices seem so routine, able to blend in with the minutiae of everyday life, that people go years, if not lifetimes, never realizing that they've been had.

Some of the more recent phishing scams, rather than directing you to a Web page, tell you to call a supplied customer support number. When you do, either a live person or some sort of automated response unit takes down your personal data to steal your identity. In most cases the person on the other end of the line warns you that your account will be terminated or other problems will ensue if you fail to comply. In case you were wondering why law enforcement doesn't trace these numbers, the answer is that the phishers use pay phones or stolen cell phones.

Another popular phishing category is fake bank ads, such as:

Whether it's a new home or if you want to refinance the one you have?...No Problem...We can help!

Whether you want to buy a new car or refinance the one you have?...That's OK...We can help!

These ads appear in newspapers and online, bearing the names and logos of impressive-sounding financial institutions. Some of the names are fabricated; most, though, are actual small- and medium-sized banks ignorant of the schemes being perpetrated in their name.

The bank's contact number, however, is that of the schemers, who are in fact looking to collect permanent loans from you. The phone numbers they give are typically for prepaid cell phones bought in Canada. If you call, you are asked for the usual personal information. To add a flourish of authenticity, some of the perpetrators require customers to mail a "loan package" with various banking information and photocopies of their Social Security cards. Later on customers are told that they need to make an advance payment on their loan through a Western Union wire transfer to an address in Canada, identified as a "third-party consultant."

If you follow the instructions, the criminals succeed in making a double strike: they acquire some immediate cash, plus they get sufficient personal information to launch an even more rewarding identity theft.

Some legitimate banks may have you contact their loan people via a cell phone, but I haven't run across any. And banks don't ask for money to be sent to them through Western Union.

Western Union has gotten so tired of seeing its name associated with this pervasive scam that they began a public information campaign in 2005 telling people about these frauds and stating that Western Union doesn't wire funds to banks in this way.

In early 2005 NBC News decided to track down one of these banks. It chose one off the Internet, Pearl Atlantic Credit & Trust. Its advertisement offered the usual boilerplate: online banking, loans, and project financing. Deposits, naturally, were said to be insured by the FDIC. There were even headshots of the CEO and other officers. When NBC looked into the ad, it found out that the man identified as the head of the bank was a real bank president—not of Pearl Atlantic but of a bank in Oregon. He had never heard of Pearl Atlantic. Using an assumed name, an NBC reporter called the bank's number, which was in the Netherlands. An operator identifying himself as being with Pearl Atlantic answered. The reporter said she wanted to speak to someone about a loan. She was told that she had to first open an account and make a deposit—$5,000. What's more, she had to fill out a form with personal information and send a copy of her ID. Later, NBC decided to go to the Netherlands to take a look at Pearl Atlantic. The address turned out to be a court building. People at the court had never heard of Pearl Atlantic. Bank regulators told the network that no such bank existed. The website had been set up by a person using a false address in Brooklyn. Soon after NBC's inquiries, the Pearl Atlantic site vanished.

Another new scam leans on the authority of the tax people and targets employees who have recently returned from working overseas. They get a letter in the mail containing a raft of legitimate-looking tax forms and are advised that they need to fill in the checked information, including the usual range of personal and banking details. This hoax has even worked effectively with companies, who get the same spiel and are asked for information on employees of theirs who had worked abroad. Some large companies that are household names have helpfully sent out the goods on hundreds of their own workers.

It's gotten so bad that the Anti-Phishing Working Group, a coalition of technology companies, financial institutions, and law enforcement agencies that tracks these crimes, reported that in 2005 there were roughly fourteen thousand phishing attacks a month. Each attack might involve thousands or millions of e-mails.

If you're a budding phisherman, you have plenty of handy instruction to get you started. Phishing kits are sold, or even offered for free, on the Internet. They contain everything from spamming software to sample e-mails from popular banks to hosting services for phishing sites that are touted as being "bulletproof," meaning that they are nearly impossible to shut down. And at a number of websites, phishers are invited to trade tips on how to engineer effective scams.

A key reason phishing is growing exponentially is that an Internet surfer really has no foolproof way to determine if an e-mail is legitimate. Website addresses cleverly rely on legitimate-sounding names to suck in their prey. You tell me which is the true address: billing.yahoo.com or yahoo-billing.com? (It's the former.) And phishermen use computer worms that wiggle from computer to computer to dispatch fake messages, so that the original source is buried and almost impossible to find. Phishing attempts sometimes come accompanied by pop-up messages bearing the name and the logo of a legitimate company or agency. Often they'll just take the image right off the real site and duplicate it on their phony message. It's no wonder people say these messages' logos look like the real thing. They basically *are* the real thing.

A more specialized variation of phishing that has recently emerged is spearfishing. In this scam, thieves home in on a specialized audience rather than send out mass e-mails. Often it will be the employees of one particular company—Ford workers, say, or Verizon employees—and the fake message supposedly originates from an executive of the company, usually from human resources or payroll. To demonstrate the danger of spearfishing, a teacher and security expert at West Point sent out e-mails to five hundred cadets informing them of a problem with their grades and asking them to click on a link to verify that their results were correct. More than 80 percent did. They got a notice that they had been duped and ought to be more cautious.

Now Enter the Pharmers

Phishing is done out in the open. You can see the phishing line; the trick is to know that it's not real. A more insidious method to capture computer-stored information over the Internet is *pharming,* or the practice of planting malicious software either on a server computer or on your own personal computer.

One way of looking at it is, phishing is nontechnical intrusion. It's a con. Pharming is technical intrusion.

The more ambitious pharming attacks go after the central server computers where genuine websites reside. Then when you type in the address of a genuine site on your browser, you get dispatched to a fraudulent one. Most often the pharming software gets onto these servers through a Trojan horse, embedded within an innocuous piece of software.

Consider Troj/Bank Ash-A, a piece of malicious software. When you visit, say, a bank website, the pharming software hijacks your browser and displays a fake log-on page that is a perfect replica of the real thing. When you type in your account information, it gets recorded and sent to a remote computer belonging to an identity thief.

Domain naming systems (DNS) are hierarchical databases that translate numerical Internet protocol (IP) addresses into human-friendly names. They are essentially large directories of common names—eBay, Amazon, Microsoft—and IP-specific addresses that you never see. It's a convenience, but it's also a weak link in the Internet infrastructure. When you try to reach an Internet site, your request first bounces off a DNS server somewhere. Changing the DNS record is the most efficient way to steal identities that course across cyberspace. Hackers can hijack a domain and redirect traffic from a legitimate site to a fraudulent one.

Often thieves poison DNS servers by impersonating an official who has the authority to change the destination of a domain name. Still others do it through software vulnerability. Just looking at the address bar of your Internet browser won't tell you that you've been hijacked.

A less sophisticated tactic is to register domain names whose addresses resemble those of popular sites. I'm talking about something as subtle as using a *1* instead of a lowercase *L* to disguise the phony site.

Pharmers also use Trojan horses to enter personal computers

and manipulate the browser cache, which is where copies of Web pages are stored so they don't have to be reloaded every time you visit them. They can manipulate your cache without your knowing it, and it's very hard to detect. What's more, thieves can pharm by infecting personal computers with a virus, so that when the user types in a Web address, the virus will send him to the pharmer's fake site, where he can steal all personal information that gets typed in.

How do Trojan horses invade your computer? They can do it whenever you download something. Crooks find ways to attach them to the free downloads popular with consumers, especially the pornography and gambling files that are pervasive on the Internet. They hide them on commonly visited websites or stick them inside e-mail attachments. Or they may be on software CDs or floppy disks that you receive and install on your computer—little unsuspected gifts that keep on giving to identity thieves.

Let's Hack People

Rather than tangle with computers, many professional thieves prefer to hack into people themselves. If I want information that's contained in a bank's database, I don't have to break into the database. All I have to do is sit in front of a bank where people are smoking, walk up to someone, and ask where they work in the bank. Then I say, "How would you like to make a lot of money? Give me certain information off the screen, and I'll give you five thousand dollars."

Twenty-five years ago, if you did that to ten people, two would say yes and eight would report you to their boss or to the police. People had more ethics and character then. Now, if people think they can get away with something, it's okay.

Don't think for a moment that it's shady-looking people or

those with a criminal mind who are willing to sell private information. Often it's simply someone who just doesn't feel that he or she makes enough money and doesn't think that disclosing this sort of information can lead to any real harm. I heard of one person who had a degree in criminal justice—who was selling credit histories from a credit union. Yes, it's a new world that we live in.

Bank of America, Wachovia, and Commerce Bank of New Jersey were all victimized by someone who simply went in and solicited employees to pull up customers' files on the screen—not steal anything—and jot the information on a Post-It in return for ten dollars a name. The person who bought the names resold them for $150 each to collection agencies and law firms that were looking for assets of people and to who knows who else. The individual made more than $4 million.

In Tacoma, Washington, a young couple in their twenties stole more than $1 million using identities that they bought from teenagers, who gave up the information on their own parents. Talk about inculcating the right values in our kids.

Sure, I'll Answer Your Questions

You would be surprised how much sensitive and valuable information crooks can con out of people without having to pay for it and without being turned in by an honest employee. It never fails to astound me the questions that intelligent people will answer about themselves to perfect strangers, given the right pretext.

How often have you been approached on the street by some fresh-faced young person representing himself as an employee of a poll company who just wanted to ask you a couple of quick questions? Or someone willing to sign you up for a free trial subscription to some newspaper or magazine, if you just write down a few things on this card? Do you think twice, or do you go along, to help out with the poll or to obtain the free magazine?

Most of these undertakings are undoubtedly genuine, but not all. A clear giveaway is if the person asks for your Social Security number. You've probably handed it out so many times in so many commonplace interactions that the request doesn't make you suspicious—which is exactly what the bogus poll-takers are banking on.

I learned about a scary experiment in trustworthiness from *Infosecure*, a newsletter written for the worldwide security printing industry.

Infosecurity Europe, a legitimate company that represents security firms in Europe, decided to try to find out firsthand what sort of information consumers were willing to relay to survey-takers who buttonholed them on the street. Three Infosecurity employees posed as interviewers conducting a survey on theater attendance. Well-groomed and dressed in business attire, they were chosen for their winning personalities. As a clever inducement, they told the people they approached that if they would take the time to answer just a few simple questions, they would receive a voucher to see a play at a local theater.

The deal was good enough that people willingly gave their names, addresses, telephone numbers, and date of birth. They were assured that all that personal data was necessary so that the research company could prove that the interviews had taken place and had not been invented.

Then the interviewers would take it a step further and pour on the charm: "Did you ever have any acting experience yourself?" And someone would respond, "No, I majored in engineering at MIT, before returning to England." Now the interviewers knew their school, which banks sometimes use to confirm identity.

The interviewers would then ask, "Say, you know, a lot of actors pick their stage names by combining pet names and their mother's maiden name. Just for fun, what would you make your stage name?" In that way, they would nail down another common bank security check, as well as an all-too-common password.

How successful were the interviewers? Over the course of a single day, they rounded up personal information on 180 people. Nine out of ten whom they approached cooperated. And guess what— identity thieves do just this sort of thing. In a 2005 survey conducted in San Francisco, VeriSign, an Internet security company, asked nearly three hundred consumers whether they would be willing to reveal their computer passwords in exchange for a $3 coupon at Starbucks. A stunning 85 percent handed over their passwords, or at least gave hints about them (my pet's name, my birthday). One person blithely remarked that he used the same password for all his security purposes, saying it was "the key to my life," then gave it up for a free latte. Would you trade the keys to your house for a coffee? Then why trade your identity?

So the next time some survey-taker or pollster stops you on the street, tell them you're late for an appointment with your astrologer.

Forget One Name at a Time—I'll Take a Million

One day a California man wrote a check to a local pizza place. The next morning the pizza store was robbed of all the cash and checks from the previous day. The man thereby became a victim of identity theft. As is so often the case, his check contained all the identifying information that a thief needed.

So robbery works. But that was penny-ante stuff.

An employee of a Sacramento processor of insurance payments was driving over to the bank to store a backup hard drive there for security reasons. It contained the names, addresses, and Social Security numbers of about 95,000 individuals. The hard drive was stashed in a satchel with his gym gear. On the way he stopped outside his accountant's office and locked the car. He was gone for all of ten minutes. In that brief time a thief smashed the rear window of the car and stole the bag and the identities. It can happen that fast, that easily.

This robbery was actually bush league too.

Data heists are far and away the most efficient means ever devised for thieves to gather leads. This way they can obtain names and personal information not one or two at a time but hundreds of thousands, if not millions, at a time. They allow for fraud on a monumental scale and their frequency is growing at an alarming pace.

In 2005 alone there were these large heists that we know about:

✴ ChoicePoint, a big data warehouse, erringly released personal information to identity thieves who were posing as legitimate debt collectors and insurance agents. They wasted no time in stealing 162,000 individual files and used at least 750 people to commit fraud.

✴ LexisNexis, the collector and seller of consumer information, admitted that more than 300,000 of its files had been swiped.

✴ Time Warner, the giant media company, "lost" a container the size of a picnic cooler that contained forty computer backup tapes bearing the names and Social Security numbers of 600,000 current and former workers and outside contractors, along with details on dependents and beneficiaries. A storage company that Time Warner had hired said the container went missing while being transported. Time Warner said it could not rule out foul play. Indeed.

* Bank of America said that it had "misplaced" backup tapes containing the records of 1.2 million federal employees, including U.S. senators and congresspeople, while they were being transferred to a backup data center. The information came from a federal government program that used Visa cards for government travel and procurement.

* The San Jose Medical Group said that the financial and medical records of almost 185,000 current and former patients were put at risk when the building was broken into and two computers housing the information were stolen. Not long before the theft, the group had begun encrypting the information because of fear of identity theft. Alas, it hadn't finished the job.

* A hacker who broke into the system of DSW Shoe Warehouse got hold of the records of credit card transactions at 108 shoe stores for some 1.4 million customers. Among the victims was the head of the Federal Trade Commission, the main agency charged with battling identity theft.

* At the University of California at Berkeley, someone swiped a laptop computer from the graduate school admissions office. It contained the personal information of 98,000 graduate students and applicants. Less than six months earlier, an attacker had broken into Berke-

ley computers and scooped up records on 600,000 students, faculty, and alumni.

✳ A computer with files harboring the names and Social Security numbers of 70,000 current and former workers at Ford Motor Company was stolen.

✳ Marriott International, the hotel chain, said that backup computer tapes in the Florida office of its time-share unit were missing. They contained the personal information of more than 200,000 people.

✳ CardSystems Solutions, a big credit card payment processor, said that computer hackers may have compromised the personal data of more than 40 million cardholders— that's right, 40 million, the largest number I've heard— most of them MasterCard and Visa customers.

✳ The thefts failed to abate in 2006, and got ever more disturbing. In May, a mid-level data analyst at the Veterans Affairs agency foolishly took home a laptop computer and external hard drive to work on a project, something he had been doing regularly for years. He lived in a Maryland neighborhood that had been plagued by a string of burglaries. Sure enough, a robber broke into his house and swiped the computer. It happened to contain the names and Social Security numbers of a whopping 17.5 million veterans, everyone who had served and been discharged since the mid-1970s. Nervous veterans, their identities suddenly thrust into play, howled their outrage at the government's lax safeguards, and I don't blame them. Nearly two months later, the FBI recovered the laptop and said it didn't think the files had been accessed, but who knows?

These data heists have become so commonplace that they happen more or less once a day. Privacy Rights Clearinghouse estimated that there were 113 major data intrusions in 2005, putting more than 52 million Americans at risk for identity theft. Half of them occurred at colleges and university-affiliated medical centers—places where scads of poorly secured data are scattered throughout their campuses.

The number of identities stolen in the ChoicePoint case was lower than some of these other thefts, but this case was particularly frightening. Here's a company, based in Alpharetta, Georgia, that most people have never heard of. Few people, in fact, had any idea such a company even existed. Yet it not only exists but happens to compile and maintain personal profiles on virtually every consumer in the United States. You're in there. I'm in there. It turns around and sells this information to employers, marketing companies, landlords, and dozens of government agencies—a grand total of more than 100,000 customers. On any given day its database contains an incredible 19 billion public records, everything including sex-offender lists, driving records, and FBI lists of most wanted criminals. It sounds to me like the number-one destination for an identity thief to visit.

The police suspected that numerous thieves were party to the caper. They managed to apprehend one of them, a Nigerian who was cornered at a California copy shop where he had faxed an application for information. He had five cell phones on him, four of them in other people's names. He had established more than a dozen commercial mailbox addresses. When cops sorted through the unopened mail piled up at those addresses, they found bags loaded with financial statements and credit card applications that had been redirected from scores of individuals in towns and cities all around the country. Welcome to the big leagues.

Between nosy washer warranties, dog pound questionnaires, and computer disks tumbling off trucks, your private information is vulnerable in a million different ways, limited only by the ingenuity of the thieves. So who's gathering all this material to rip you off? It's a much larger universe than you've been led to believe.

4

It Could Be Public Enemy Number One
or It Could Be Grandma

In 2004 and 2005 a college professor in the Midwest told his freshman and sophomore students that when they submitted their exams, they were to write their name, Social Security number, and date of birth at the top of the page. Finding nothing unusual in the request, hundreds of his students dutifully obliged. The professor was well loved—and he loved his students, especially their untainted credit standing. He proceeded to charge more than $200,000 to credit cards in their names that he fraudulently obtained using the information that they had trustingly provided him. They hadn't even graduated from college, and their credit was a mess. But they had gotten a brutal early lesson in the criminal workings of the real world.

Yes, even your Latin or anthropology professor these days might be an identity thief.

It Beats Bibles

A lot of people have a gross misconception about identity thieves. They think they're shady guys sitting in a dilapidated hotel room in Brooklyn who pick names at random. They think they're hardened criminals on drugs or penny-ante crooks looking to steal their identity to get a credit card. Sometimes they are, but most of the time they aren't.

More than any other crime, identity theft is an equal opportunity employer. Fortunately for society, not everyone is a murderer, and not everyone is inclined to break into people's homes and assault them. But an astonishingly diverse group of individuals are perfectly comfortable making at least a part-time living as identity thieves. They are people of all ages, all races, both sexes, all cultures, all religions, educated and uneducated, straight arrows and deviants, blue collar and white collar. It's truly a crime of the masses.

On Monday nights Jay Leno always does a hilarious bit featuring amusing clippings that viewers send him from daily newspapers and restaurant menus. One night he displayed a classified ad from a local newspaper soliciting people for "Part-time work out of your home. Good income. Identity theft." Well, why not? It beats Amway and selling Bibles door to door.

Given that the opportunity is great and the risk is low, almost anyone might be willing to give identity theft a try. After all, it's not a violent crime. You don't have to carry a gun. You don't even have to face your victim. This last factor may explain why, unlike most crimes, identity theft appeals to a great many women. According to a 2004 study by Judith Collins, a professor at Michigan State University, in more than a thousand randomly selected identity theft cases, roughly half the culprits were women. Her conclusion was that men are apt to be higher risk-takers than women, but since identity theft entails so little risk, a lot of unethical women find it alluring.

I'm not suggesting that everyone is capable of becoming a diehard identity thief, whose only source of income is credit that belongs to someone else. There are plenty of people like that, but there are also countless people who, under the right circumstances, will dabble in identity theft, try a quick score, and then return to word processing or minding the car wash. To some people, identity theft seems so harmless that it doesn't strike them as much more than a prank.

So the perpetrators are everyone from computer-handy kids to career criminals. It could be organized crime or your father-in-law. It could be a serial killer or Aunt Marge. It could be the teenager next door, amusing himself during the lull between doing his calculus homework and watching NCAA basketball. It could be a low-tech person who breaks into mailboxes or a high-tech person who breaks into online bank accounts.

It's the Girl Who Just Served Your Omelet

A twenty-three-year-old waitress at a popular restaurant on Fenwick Island, Delaware, was arrested for using a hand-held credit card reader, known as a skimmer, to steal identities. The device reads and records the information on magnetic stripes, thus allowing criminals to make fake cards. The police said that the waitress had copied about fifty cards. She explained that at a party a Russian man who set up the scheme approached her. He paid her $10 for Visa and MasterCard numbers and $15 for American Express. The bounty for the latter was higher because, he told her, they were harder to counterfeit.

Skimmers of this sort are everywhere nowadays, not only because they work so effectively but because so many places that never took credit cards now do. McDonald's and other fast-food places accept them. In some cities cab drivers take them.

Which means that anyone who serves you a drink, takes you to the airport, or performs any other service for you could be a potential identity thief. Wilfrid Sheed, a noted writer who lives in North Haven, Long Island, is in his mid-seventies. He and his wife needed some help around the house. Through an acquaintance they met a man who was willing to do odd jobs for them. The man put in an air conditioner and did some other tasks, and before long he moved in with the Sheeds. He drove them places and bought groceries for them. And while he was at it, he helped himself to their identities. He withdrew money from their accounts and opened new accounts in Sheed's name, using them to buy electronic goods that he then sold on the street in New York.

Do you think you're safe when you're being wheeled into a hospital? Nurses and orderlies are not beneath trying to earn extra money at your expense. The environment lends itself perfectly. A Social Security number often serves as a patient's medical identification number, and when you enter the hospital, your guard is down. Your mind is on your failing liver or your clogged arteries, not on crime. In early 2005 the University of Chicago hospitals acknowledged that a former employee had swiped the identities of close to a hundred patients. Similar occurrences have taken place in other cities. One ring of thieves in New Jersey specifically preyed on the terminally ill, realizing that they were unlikely to be closely watching their credit.

Some scam artists pose as hospital workers or nursing home

employees, carrying clipboards and even wearing true-life white hospital coats. They ask patients to verify information about themselves that they then scribble down on their pads.

Teens and Grandmas

I don't know who the youngest identity thief on record is, but people do take up the crime at an early age. A nineteen-year-old Drexel University student sent out online invitations to a stock forum where people could sample a new stock-charting tool. The tool was actually a software program called The Bear that secretly monitored the keystrokes of the computer user. Armed with the stolen log-in and password of one brokerage account, he made $46,000 trading options of Cisco Systems.

In 2004 Alec Scott Papierniak, a twenty-year-old college student from Mankato, Minnesota, pleaded guilty to wire fraud. He sent e-mails containing a security update supposedly from PayPal. Once someone installed the program—and more than 150 people did—it reported their PayPal user names and passwords to Papierniak, who used the information to reward himself to the tune of $35,000.

Age doesn't necessarily make you wiser, only more ambitious. Thus we have Helen Carr, a grandmother who was living with her own eighty-year-old mother in Akron, Ohio. From the comfort of her home, Carr collaborated on a phishing scheme with a man named George Patterson in Pennsylvania; she had met him in an Internet chat room and only spoke to him over the Internet. (In a scam within a scam, Carr led Patterson to believe that she was a slim blonde in her twenties named Kristi. Actually she was an overweight fifty-five-year-old with blond highlights. She had sent Patterson a photo—of her niece.)

Carr and Patterson began by sending out fake "InstaKiss messages" to AOL subscribers from "secret admirers." To see the InstaKiss, a recipient had to type his screen name and password into a form—which was forwarded to Carr and Patterson. They used the information to log on to AOL and deployed spamming software known as Green Eggs and Spam to launch a full-scale phishing attack.

They sent out mass e-mails cleverly disguised as coming from AOL's Security Department. The messages drily informed the victims that AOL's last attempt to bill their credit card had been declined and that unless they supplied AOL with updated credit card and account information, their account, alas, would be terminated. To furnish the information, they were directed to click on a link that took them to a website dressed up as the "AOL Billing Center." Anything entered there was promptly forwarded to an e-mail account belonging to Carr and her pal.

Who knows how long the scam might have gone on? But one of the marks turned out to be an FBI agent in Virginia. Handily enough, he was also a computer crimes specialist. He started an investigation, and both conspirators were nabbed and pleaded guilty to their wrongdoing in 2004.

The Nerd from College? Hang Up

What are friends for, if not to steal your identity? Most friends, of course, wouldn't stoop that low, but some would. According to a study by Javelin Strategy & Research, a California consulting firm, in more than a quarter of cases of identity theft, the victim knew the thief—and he was a family member, friend, neighbor, or live-in employee.

You ought to be especially alert if a friend you haven't heard from since the last fraternity beer bash in 1974 contacts you. One of the most popular identity theft scams is to call up an old college buddy and do a little bit more than reminisce. The crook will phone you and say, "Hey, Robert, it's Bill Black."

"Bill Black? I haven't seen you since college."

"Yeah, I was going through the yearbook and saw your picture, and I thought I'd give you a call. How are you doing?"

"Doing great."

"So what are you doing now?"

"Oh, I'm the CEO of XYZ Company in New York."

"Oh, really, CEO." The guy's writing this down. Then he asks, "So listen, you married Helen Jones, who you went to school with?"

"Oh, no, I married a local girl, Karen Johnson."

"I see. Now I always thought your birthday was in May, and I was going to send you a card."

"No, my birthday is in November. November sixteenth."

"November. Let me make a note of that."

By the time this little out-of-the-blue conversation is over, Bill Black has weaseled enough information from his old classmate to seize his credit.

It's Not the Butler, It's the Window Washer

A great deal of identity theft starts with a person who sits next to you at work. Or two doors down. Or on the ninth floor, in the credit department. Or down the hall in technical support. Or working the squeegee outside your window. I'm talking about the inside job.

I've seen a tremendous increase in the number of identity thieves who wouldn't normally be considered the criminal type—namely, people sitting around at work muttering to themselves, "I'm desperate to buy a car, but I've got a bankruptcy on my credit, so no one's going to loan me any money. But I know Bob in the mailroom. He's sixty years old and has worked here for fifteen years, so he's probably got great credit and likely never checks it. I'm going to buy a car under Bob's name. He'll never know, and I'll make the payments every month on time. Then at the end of the note, I'll already be Bob, so I'll just sign the car title over to me."

A nurse with shaky credit who worked at an Oklahoma hospital went ahead and stole the identity of one of the pediatricians on staff. In a busy two weeks, while still getting pills for patients and checking blood pressures, she used the doctor's identity to obtain thirty credit cards, nine cell phones, a motorcycle, a car, and a spiffy wardrobe.

It's hard to know how much information stolen from workplaces gets used for identity theft, since so much of it isn't reported out of embarrassment. What's more, a lot of companies aren't even aware that information is missing. But there's no question it's a dazzling amount.

Judith Collins and her students at Michigan State, in their examination of identity theft complaints that had been filed with the police, called or wrote these victims and asked them, "How did the person get the information to steal your identity?" Of those who knew, a shocking 70 percent responded that the thief obtained the information from a low-level employee who sold it to somebody else. Trust me, people are approaching the cleaning staff somewhere pretty much every day.

Businesses used to worry about shrinkage—employees pilfering sweaters and toasters and, of course, actual cash—but data that can be used for identity theft is now a much more valuable commodity. Most inside jobs, Collins found, take place at financial or health care companies, since that's where so much personal data is stockpiled. Here's another surprise Collins turned up—a lot of those identities were stolen by the business owner himself.

Colleges commonly employ students in low-level jobs as part of their student-aid programs. Frequently these students have ready access to a wide amount of personal data. Sometimes they help themselves to it for nefarious gain. In 2003, for instance, a student employee at the University of Texas stole 55,000 Social Security numbers. You can be sure it wasn't for a class assignment.

Some gangs of criminals even place people in jobs specifically so they can gather information for the ring to use to steal identities. The Treasury Department has warned banks about the practice of organized crime planting people in low-level teller jobs at branches so that they can abscond with personal information.

A janitor at a Queens military base stole the identifications of 150 soldiers who were serving in Iraq and other overseas posts, then got credit cards in their names and bought expensive suits and jeans. He wasted little time—he had worked on the base all of three days.

I went to the mall with a friend once, and we stopped by a phone company kiosk so that he could change his phone service. A teenage employee said that he needed my friend's driver's license and credit card, both of which he dutifully copied. Then he filled out a form that required my friend's Social Security number, birth date, bank, bank location, and account number. I couldn't believe all the information he wanted. I was expecting him to ask for his shoe size and the name of the first girl he kissed.

I asked this seventeen-year-old, "What do you do with that piece of paper and those copies?"

"I fax them to our home office," he said.

"And once you've faxed them, what do you do with them?"

"Uh, just throw them away."

"You don't shred them or anything?"

"No."

In other words, if I'm a janitor at the mall, I could build up an incredible business every night just by emptying that trash can and selling the contents.

Just think of all the low-level workers with access to enormous amounts of sensitive information. Most of them are honest, but it only takes a few malevolent ones to compromise a great many innocent consumers.

In late 2004 thirty-five-year-old Philip Cummings pleaded guilty to what was thought to be the biggest identity theft in U.S. history. He was a help-desk worker at Teledata Communications, a Long Island computer software company that provided banks with computerized access to credit information databases. He sold passwords and codes for downloading consumer credit reports to crooks for $30 apiece. More than ten thousand reports were stolen, and the theft in these identities amounted to $50 million.

Workers of all stripes are doing the same thing. A human resources worker at Starbucks was indicted for stealing employee identities that he peddled for $150 per name. A Washington Air National Guard clerk was indicted in Seattle for stealing names and Social Security numbers of military personnel. An IRS worker was convicted of stealing and selling the personal information of taxpayers and their dependents. A woman who worked in the payroll department of a cell phone company sold the identities of more than a hundred workers to a thief who used them to hack into their online accounts and transfer money. A former AOL employee stole 92 million e-mail screen names and passwords from the provider's subscriber list and sold them for $28,000.

It goes on and on, with health care workers, clerks at motor vehicle departments, tellers at banks, and department store sales-people. Your information is everywhere, and workers with little if any security clearance know where the stuff is—and have the means and authority to get to it.

Bear in mind all the other people who visit workplaces, who aren't full-time employees and may not even be logged in in any formal fashion: casual workers, outside contractors, deliverymen, ap-plicants arriving for interviews—and people who mistakenly (or maybe not so mistakenly) got the wrong address.

The handyman of a dentist stole a patient's information. He bought a condo and a BMW and used the victim's HMO to get med-ical service.

In the aftermath of 9/11, a program was set up in New York to track the lingering health effects of the terrorist attack on the myriad rescue workers and volunteers who had been exposed to the smoldering pit in downtown Manhattan. A great many of these indi-viduals were heroes in the best sense of the word. That made all the more disturbing the news that in late 2005 a computer containing in-formation about them had been stolen. Letters went out to the eleven thousand participants in the health project, cautioning them that they might be at risk for identity theft. The letter stressed that the data was coded and that a password was necessary to get at the mate-rial saved on the computer. But getting past codes and passwords is child's play for a semisophisticated computer hacker. The database harbored relatively little health information on the cops and steel-workers—material that was of no interest to identity thieves anyway. But it contained ample amounts of personal information that others could use to adopt the identities of these heroes.

How did the computer get pilfered? It was taken from a hospital office in East Harlem. Possible suspects? The police were looking for a painter who had been doing some touchup work in the office.

Look Out for Aunt Sadie

One of the saddest aspects of identity theft is that it is often the handiwork of family members—demonstrable evidence that a drastic breakdown in values has poisoned modern society. A recent report by the Federal Trade Commission concluded that in roughly 9 percent of all cases the perpetrator is a relative. That equates to 900,000 cases—an amazing number. And when it's family pulling the caper, the emotional wallop for the victim is all the worse. If you can't trust your own relatives, who can you trust?

A California man opened a letter one day from the Treasury Department and was shocked to learn that the $5,000 federal tax refund he was counting on had been instead turned over to the child support division of the county district attorney's office. The same letter also threatened to intercept all federal payments going to him. Since he was employed by the navy, that meant that he might soon no longer get paid. It seems that his half-brother, who had made a mess of his own life, had now chosen to make a mess of his relative's. Using his half-brother's Social Security number, the thief established a cable TV account that he defaulted on, then followed up by posing as his brother to land several jobs. Meanwhile, he owed more than $75,000 in back child support. When the district attorney's office got involved, it followed the trail of the Social Security number to his navy half-brother.

It's Even Mom and Dad

A college student in Kansas, who didn't even own any credit cards, took advantage of an offer for a free look at her credit report, just to see what it was all about. She was surprised to discover a credit card listed on the report with a sizable balance that hadn't been paid in more than two months. Mystified and a little alarmed, she did what any confused child would do—she called her mother for comfort and advice. That was the wrong place to go. Her mother, badly overextended on her own credit, was the one who had stolen her daughter's identity.

Another mother took her seven-year-old daughter to the bank to open a checking account for the young girl, marking her entry into the world of finance. The bank took a look in the computer and said sorry, the girl has a bad credit report, we can't serve her. It turned out that her father had been using the child's Social Security number to open credit accounts that he then exhausted in wild spending binges.

A teenage boy went to collect his first paycheck ever, only to find it garnished because authorities said he was long overdue on child support payments. They were actually his father's child support payments. The man had stolen his son's identity.

This kind of thing used to be just about unheard of, but more and more parents are employing the Social Security numbers of their own children to create fake accounts that often go undetected for years, sometimes until the children are grown and have children themselves. It's horrifying, but it happens. The appeal of theft is a mighty opiate.

You would think that minors would be relatively immune to this crime. Generally they can't get credit cards, because the law specifies that a person isn't legally able to be held to a contract until he's eighteen. But since when does the law matter? Issuers of credit, in their haste to rack up ever more business, frequently accept a Social Security number and name at face value, without demanding proof of age. And if they do want proof, identity thieves have no trouble coming up with a counterfeit birth certificate or driver's license. Once one piece of credit is established, others follow smoothly, building on one another.

When it comes to committing identity theft, diabolical parents have a double edge. They already know their children's names, birth dates, and Social Security numbers. They can destroy mail that could alert other family members to the fishy activity. And children, even when they learn the nasty truth, are usually loath to call the cops on their own mother or father. One mother, presumably not wanting to play favorites, fraudulently used the identities of all five of her children. It was the grandmother who turned her in.

These cases are the modern-day equivalent of a parent stealing a kid's piggy bank off his dresser—only the sums are much larger, and the texture of the misdeeds a lot creepier.

These frauds can leave blemishes on a child's credit that can interfere with his attempts to get a job or borrow money. Late payments remain lodged on credit reports for seven years. One college student who had been fleeced by an identity thief found her credit score ruined. She felt humiliated, especially since she was a finance major.

The emotional scars left on children don't readily heal. Financial abuse may not trigger the severe psychological repercussions that rape or other sexual abuse does, but a child still feels indelibly wounded by those she loves and counts on to shield her from the myriad menaces of the world. Victimized children can grow up to find themselves unusually suspicious of everyone and thus have a hard time establishing enduring relationships or even marrying, all because of this early breach, and that's a far greater tragedy than any financial loss. Often children need professional counseling to be reassured that they were not somehow at fault.

Identity Theft, Inc.

At the other end of the spectrum from Mom or Dad are, increasingly, the criminal rings. Make no mistake, identity theft is a business. It's a profession. You can build a company around it. And people have done exactly that.

Authorities have come across numerous criminal identity theft organizations that are run like hierarchical businesses. Some of them carry names like Darkprofits, Shadowcrew, and Carderplanet, and they are usually headed by Eastern Europeans or Russians. They carry huge inventories of stolen identities, and criminals shopping for names and digits can easily locate them on the Internet. Worried about security themselves, these companies have their own rules to screen out cops. New traffickers, for instance, are often asked to prove their evil background by presenting samples of stolen data.

Numerous phishers have impersonated EarthLink, the major Internet service provider. When that company tried to run them down, it discovered a flurry of e-mails originating from computers in Eastern Europe, especially Russia, as well as Asia. The assumption was that they were criminal rings. Other schemes have been traced to Romania, where in one instance Romanian authorities arrested more than a hundred people in an eBay impersonation fraud. It had been their inspired idea to contact people who had lost out in online auctions and tell them that similar merchandise was available at even lower prices, as long as they handed over their information.

Romania has become such an important source of identity theft rings that in 2003 the government enacted one of the harshest laws against online theft. A thief can go to jail for as long as fifteen years, which is twice the maximum sentence for rape. But the police have a difficult time keeping up with the burgeoning cases.

Some of these networks are organized almost like the Mafia, with the equivalent of wiseguys and bosses, though they also mimic publicly traded corporations in their structures and sophistication.

These businesses even outsource some of their grunt work. They place classified ads in newspapers and on employment websites soliciting people who want to earn money working out of their homes as "correspondence managers" or other vague positions. (Naturally, the networks pay for the ads with stolen credit cards.) All the enlistees have to do is to accept deliveries of packages containing merchandise like video cameras and computers, slap a fresh mailing label on them, and reship them to corporate headquarters, usually someplace in Romania, Russia, or the Philippines. They're paid $25 to $50 per package—easy money no matter how you look at it.

The reshippers may think of themselves as correspondence managers, but they're actually unwitting identity theft "mules," the equivalent of couriers who stealthily move cocaine and other drugs across borders. Merchants are often suspicious of expensive purchases that get shipped overseas, so identity theft businesses use mules to evade detection and steer clear of law enforcement.

Thousands of people are thought to have been recruited for this new form of stay-at-home work. Some are enticed on singles websites, wooed with boxes of chocolates. Little niceties do work. Identity theft has gotten so businesslike and brazen that a conference for identity thieves was called in Kiev to draw fresh blood into the field. The insurance industry has its sales conferences; swimming pool makers have theirs; is it really any wonder that identity thieves now do the same thing?

5

What Your Duplicate Is Doing as You

In early 2003 a seventy-two-year-old British man named Derek Bond, a retired engineer, grandfather of six, Rotarian, and wine enthusiast, was arrested in South Africa, where he had been on a wine-tasting vacation with his wife. Told that the FBI had identified him as a wanted fugitive, he was imprisoned in a Durban jail. He was fingered, the authorities informed him, for masterminding a marketing scheme, supposedly intended to market telephone calling cards, that fleeced more than two hundred investors of millions of dollars. Though he insistently professed his innocence, the police were convinced that they had their man. For three weeks Bond was forced to sleep on a concrete floor. So distraught was he by what had happened to him that his appetite vanished, and he lost weight by the day.

After twenty days, he caught a break. The real culprit, an identity thief, was nabbed in a Las Vegas hotel room. Bond was released, whereupon his mood and his appetite picked up. It turned out that the crook had been using Bond's identity since as far back as 1989. Oddly enough, they were the same age.

If you think identity theft involves just credit card fraud and obtaining fraudulent loans, it doesn't—it's far more diabolical. Once a crook has inhabited your life, he no longer limits his horizons but tries every angle both to enrich himself and to deflect attention when he violates the law. Actually, the scariest thing to me about identity theft is not the financial fraud, as bad as that is, but the possibility that someone will go out and commit a crime in your name. I mean a heavy-duty crime, like drug trafficking, rape, armed robbery, or even murder.

In simpler days, criminals used to make up names in order to dupe the law when they committed a crime and sneaked across a border. Now they steal names of real people and use them instead. It works out a lot better for them. In most cases the police do only so much to verify an identity. Suppose a crook gives a name and shows what appears to be a valid driver's license to back it up. The police book him under that name. He then makes bail or gets released on his own recognizance. He'll never return to face the charges, and the warrant goes out for some guy playing catch in the backyard with his son who never even had a speeding ticket. The thief has beaten the system, and now the system beats you.

Cases like the one affecting Mr. Bond seem extraordinary, but they're becoming more commonplace. A survey by the Identity Theft Data Clearinghouse in 2000, in fact, discovered that 12 percent of identity theft victims were the unhappy recipients of a wrongful criminal record. So numerous are the incidents that some district attorney's offices have instituted special procedures to address them, called identity hearings.

So a man was sitting at home one evening relaxing with his children in Janesville, Wisconsin. The doorbell rang, and when he opened the door, the police arrested him for cocaine possession with intent to distribute. They slapped on the handcuffs and took him away. Not until he spent two days in jail did the cops realize that the man was a victim of identity theft. This false criminal record hounded him for years. He got fired from a job for lying about his criminal record. He was laid off from another job and was denied unemployment benefits because of his criminal record. His driver's license was suspended because of his criminal record. But the criminal record wasn't his—it was the identity thief's.

A fourth-grade teacher in San Diego casually opened a letter one day and discovered to her horror that a warrant for her arrest had been issued in a nearby county on a prostitution charge. The real hooker was a teenager she had mentored as a volunteer in a foster care facility. She wasn't caught, though, and additional prostitution warrants were issued in other California counties, as well as in Arizona, Florida, and Nebraska. Needless to say, the teacher was shamed beyond belief.

A man was stopped by the Aurora, Colorado, police after passing through a yellow light in the process of turning red—one of those marginal calls that we all experience. Given the ambiguous circumstances, he hoped to get a reprimand and be on his way. After running the man's identification through the computer, however, the police officer directed him to step outside his car. When he got out, the cop proceeded to turn him around, handcuff him, haul him down to the station, and throw him in jail.

The man worked selling software for a government contractor and had never had a run-in of consequence with the law. When he asked for an explanation, he was told curtly that he was wanted on two felonies.

Two years earlier someone had gone into a rental place and signed for $10,000 in computer equipment and furniture. As proof of who he was, he handed over a driver's license—the arrested man's driver's license. The crook was about fifty pounds lighter and five inches taller than the man pictured on the ID, and he had a rash of tattoos, but none of that seemed to catch the interest of the rental staff. He arranged to have the purchases delivered to his apartment, a different address from the one on the license. Unsurprisingly, he never paid for the goods. He happened to be a career criminal, always looking for the next dodge.

The innocent victim had lost his driver's license not long before the crime, but he had reported it and had it replaced. Little good that did him. It cost him several thousand dollars to clear his name.

Thieves sometimes do make a bum choice. A certain James Perry had been living in Florida, where he was plagued by a string of drunken driving arrests. He moved to Connecticut, and to clear up his driver's license problem, he assumed the identity of his next-door neighbor. One day he got picked up for disorderly conduct. When the police ran his name through the system—the name, that is, of his neighbor—it turned out the guy was a convicted sex offender and had neglected to register his status. This slapdash case reminded me of the 1950s film *Across the Bridge,* in which Rod Steiger plays a crooked financier on the lam who switches identities with a stranger he meets on a train, only to discover that the stranger is wanted for murder. Perry, like Rod Steiger, had stolen the wrong identity.

Home? What Home?

Identity thieves have to live somewhere, so why not in your new home? You can't buy a home with somebody's credit card, but you can be approved for a loan using his credit.

A former mortgage broker in Spring Valley, South Carolina, stole the personal information of a client, a seventy-year-old man living off Social Security, and bought a house in his name with a $306,000 loan. He moved in and lived there for a year and a half without ever making a mortgage payment. Delinquent notices eventually got sent to the victim, who mistakenly thought they were for another loan that he had taken out to help his daughter buy a house in a different town. The bank made it clear that the payments were overdue for his Spring Valley home. His response was "What Spring Valley home?"

Real estate has long been a great way to make money legitimately, but it's also a great way to make money illegitimately. Late in 2005 a man was arrested in New York for stealing another man's identity and then buying a $600,000 home in Brooklyn. He had actually been living under the other man's identity for nearly a year. He started small, rounding up some credit cards and using them to make modest purchases. Things went swimmingly enough that he became emboldened and thought, why not buy a house? He had the credit cards and a false driver's license he created. He toured properties with real estate agents before choosing the one he liked. He applied for a mortgage, hired a lawyer for the closing, and completed the deal. The crook wasn't quite clever enough to cover his tracks, though; the victim was notified about being approved for the mortgage and got the police involved. The cops nabbed the guy just as he was preparing to move in. Apparently he was intending to steal money from the victim's accounts until the property had appreciated enough for him to sell it at a nice profit.

In another not atypical instance, a landlord asked a tenant if she would sign some documents the landlord needed to "help him own property." The tenant was just eighteen and naïve. She thought she was doing a good deed. Affixing her name to the documents automatically made her the co-owner of an apartment building guaranteed by a Federal Housing Administration loan. Sometime later she was refused credit because a pair of bankruptcies were staining her credit record. It seems that the landlord had filed for them in her name to prevent a foreclosure. At least she had company. The guy had also gone bankrupt in the names of numerous other tenants and employees.

One of the most pervasive scams these days begins when thieves drive around suburban neighborhoods where the elderly live and where the homes are valued at a minimum of $250,000. (Crooks don't like to waste their time unless the pickings are choice.) They spot an old man, seventy or seventy-five, raking leaves outside his home, or maybe supervising some kid he hired to rake the leaves. They jot down the address on the mailbox: 122 Elm Street or 5804 Lavender Drive. They have no name, just an address.

Then they open a wireless laptop and go to the public county records and land title records to see who lives there. Let's call the occupant Henry Parker. Any mortgage on the house? None, paid off ten years ago. Any liens? Not a one. The place is free and clear. Their eyes are getting bigger. What they've got is a fish waiting to be reeled in.

They immediately head to a local bank—the first one they come to will do—and apply for a $25,000 loan using Mr. Parker's home as the collateral. When you're borrowing less than 10 percent of the market value of a property, no appraisal is required.

Two months later this seventy-five-year-old man gets a payment booklet in the mail from a mortgage company and wonders why. It takes months and money dug out of his own pocket for him to get the problem resolved and to get that lien removed from his property. Imagine the feeling of invasion, the questioning of who could do such a cruel thing.

It can get worse. In 2003 a ring of identity thieves were caught in Queens who had conned $1 million from mortgage companies by staging phony real estate closings. They would pick a home, and one member of the ring would create false papers so he could pose as the real owner of the property. Another member would pretend to be a buyer, and the home would be fraudulently sold to him, with a mortgage obtained from a duped mortgage broker. The criminals would then divide up the bank check that was issued for the purchase of the home. Six victims found that their homes had been sold out from under them this way. One of the defrauded mortgage brokers wound up going bankrupt from the losses it incurred.

Let's All Get a Car

Another familiar application of identity theft is to sell stolen identities to people with poor credit so they can buy necessities like a car. That's the route that Kwezeta Butler took. A young Georgia woman, she turned a fondness for the obituary pages into a sideline as an identity theft ringleader. What she did—and she pleaded guilty to the caper in the summer of 2004—was to pick names out of the obits in a far-flung group of newspapers, then rely on an Internet background search company to supply her with the necessary details on these people.

She put together dead identities from California, Oklahoma, Georgia, Virginia, and Ohio. She packaged the information and sold it, at a rate of $500 to $600 per name, to people with inadequate credit who were looking to buy cars. The plot involved a crooked salesman at a car dealership in Atlanta. Butler would steer her customers to this salesman, who would accept the dead as cosigners on loans to buy cars. Before the ring was broken up, Butler had sold identities to some eighty people, and car loans totaling more than $1.5 million had been granted.

The scheme might have continued for a lot longer than it did if one of the criminals had not gotten greedy. He also went ahead and applied for a credit card in a dead man's name. The man's sister happened to learn about this peculiar event—her brother seeking a charge card after he was dead. Rather than assume it was a mistake and forget about it, she mentioned it to her son. He was a sheriff's deputy. Sensing that something was awry, he began the investigation that undid Butler.

I'll Take the Job, You Pay the Taxes

A while ago a young Chicago-area woman drove over to a nearby Target store to apply for a job. She filled out the application, left, and waited to hear back from the personnel department. Thinking herself amply qualified, she fully expected to get an affirmative response. Soon afterward she received a call from the store and was informed to her surprise that, sorry, her application had been rejected. When she asked why, she was told that it was because she already worked at the store.

As absurd as that sounded, it was, in a technical sense, true. It seems that an illegal immigrant had gotten hold of her personal information and had landed a job under the young woman's name at that very same store. In fact, the victimized woman soon learned that thirty-seven other immigrants were working at other stores under her name, easily making her one of the most productive workers in America. Just about everyone had a job as her except her.

It's an increasingly common practice for illegal immigrants to become identity thieves. In order to remain in the country, or to get official papers or jobs, they conclude that the best recourse is to steal someone else's name and make it theirs. In a widely publicized episode, Bernard Kerik, the former New York City police commissioner, abandoned his chance to become the Homeland Security head when he learned that his children's nanny was an illegal immigrant who had been working for him using somebody else's Social Security number.

Unlike other identity thieves, who tend to be selfish with stolen information, immigrants frequently share it willingly with friends and relatives so that you find yourself simultaneously employed at dozens of different jobs in scattered cities and states. That makes it devilishly difficult to straighten out the mess.

Other people steal your identity not because they want a permanent job but because they want to borrow your job for a half hour or an hour. Why? To get access to a building. They're keen to get information from your employer—such as a trade secret or a marketing plan that could assist a competitor. So they acquire the identity of an employee with the appropriate access, stroll into the building under that person's information, and make off with what they want. You could call it highly short-term identity theft.

Working Uncle Sam Over

Identity thieves always get a kick out of rounding up tax refunds, courtesy of you. No, they don't swipe your regular refund. They create an entirely new return in your name, one that calls for money back from Uncle Sam.

There is one minor obstacle here: the fact that you'll be filing a return as well. The IRS has never been receptive to two returns arriving from the same person, especially when they both call for refunds. But that's not a problem. Thieves tend to file a lot sooner than you do. Even if they don't, they'll prepare a return and then, before the IRS has time to process it, use it to get what's known as a *refund anticipation loan,* a short-term, high-interest loan against an expected refund that banks are happy to extend. The interest charges are preposterous—the annual percentage rates can exceed 700 percent. But the thief doesn't care. The loan isn't in his name. It's in your name.

The other thing is, criminals aren't choosy. They'll even prey on their own kind. Prisoners, being between jobs, generally don't file tax returns. That makes them appetizing targets. A man in Miami managed to file false federal tax returns in the names of 614 Florida prisoners, calling for more than $3 million in fraudulent refunds.

While criminals outside prison walls are scamming the ones inside, the inmates are doing the same thing. In South Carolina an inmate prepared fake W-2 forms using the names and Social Security numbers of unwitting fellow inmates. He then created ten false tax returns, heavy on deductions that meant good-sized refunds. He persuaded the mother of another inmate who was in on the plot to allow her checking account to be used to receive the refunds. It filled up fast.

They Even Want Your Magic Potions

Whatever has tangible cash value will catch the attention of identity thieves—even things like virtual battle hammers and magic shields. A recent phishing scam I read about targeted the sizable universe of participants in those multiplayer role-playing online games like City of Heroes, World of Warcraft, and Dark Age of Camelot. A phony message went out to players informing them that access to their game account was being limited because the game operator had detected "unusual activity." To restore full access and avoid being banned from the game, the person had to click on a link and provide his log-in information. What's the appeal to identity thieves, other than a chance to relax and play some games themselves?

Well, players take these elaborate virtual worlds extremely seriously. Scammers in the past tried to acquire other players' identities so that they could skip the hard work and considerable skill necessary to advance to higher levels of the games. Now something new has happened. Players have been selling necessary acquisitions to succeed at the games—various weapons, characters, and gold coins, among other goods—for hard cash. Successful players are putting potions and currency they've acquired up for auction on eBay and other online marketplaces. Incredibly enough, hundreds of millions of dollars of virtual goods are estimated to be sold each year. That's more than enough to whet the appetite of identity thieves. So they get hold of the characters and coins by adopting the identities of the players who earned them, then proceed to sell the goods themselves.

They Go Bankrupt

Crooks aren't particularly proficient at managing their finances, and being freelancers, their incomes can fluctuate a lot. Once they start relying on your credit, they draw you into all sorts of nasty outcomes.

They may get you entangled in lawsuits, like the criminal who stole a woman's identity, then rented and totaled a Thrifty rental car. Her name was on the agreement, so the rental agency sued her for it. The thief had posed as her business associate to request her credit report—and got it. The thief also went ahead and did some free-wheeling spending beyond renting that car.

If times really get tough, thieves find themselves forced to file for bankruptcy. But they'll do it under your name. After running up bills they can't afford, buying cars and homes for which they can't meet the payments, they'll choose bankruptcy in order to freeze all the liens that have accumulated and to stave off foreclosures. The bankruptcy doesn't bother them—it goes on your record.

Not long ago a woman saw a notice in the mail that was addressed to her son. She opened it and was stunned to find him being summoned to appear at a meeting of creditors that was to be conducted as part of his Chapter 13 bankruptcy case. This was rather disturbing. Her son wasn't in any debt that she was aware of. After all, he was five years old.

A sweeping new federal bankruptcy law went into effect in October 2005, designed to eliminate so-called "bankruptcies of convenience" by people who have abused their credit without ever intending to pay the bills. The law is having a perverse effect on victims of identity theft. Debtors now have to repay some of their old debt, and there are no exclusions. That means that if an identity thief runs up excessive debt in your name and files for bankruptcy, you'll be held responsible for the bills. And they call that justice!

Student Aid Without the Homework

Student loans have become a popular target for enterprising identity thieves, and why not? They're all too easy to obtain. Some thieves will get one loan and be on their way. Others get hooked.

My favorite case is the Arizona man who, between 1999 and 2003, used more than fifty identities to obtain over $300,000 in student loans and other forms of financial aid. At least most of the identities he stole weren't those of students who could have used the aid themselves. For the most part, he used the names of prisoners serving lengthy sentences. He bought the inmates' names on the Internet. (That's right. In addition to towels and snow shovels, you can purchase the names of prisoners on the Web.) Then he wrote to them, posing as a lawyer interested in assisting them in appeals. From their responses, he was able to accumulate enough information to apply for aid under their identities.

He never attended any classes at the colleges that provided the aid—places like Maricopa Community College, Mesa Community College, and Scottsdale Community College—and he steered clear of the social life. He simply showed up at the financial aid offices at the appointed times to retrieve his checks. He methodically pocketed one after the other, never raising an eyebrow, and got caught only when he made the mistake of going twice to the same aid official to get checks under two different names. It's pretty easy to fool colleges, but even they have their limits.

They'll Steal the Whole Company

For some thieves, stealing the identity of a single individual won't do. They abscond with an entire company. This little-known version of identity theft goes to show that there's no underestimating the creativity of a crook.

A couple of years ago the identity of T-Data, a small software company in New York, was lifted wholesale. Company policy was not to accept credit cards. Identity thieves, however, went ahead and created a spurious T-Data with its own website that did accept credit cards. They then established accounts with merchant processing providers—the people who transfer funds between credit card companies and businesses. Once those accounts were in place, the thieves charged purchases to the false merchant accounts. The credit card companies released payments to the processors, and they sent the money off to the bank accounts of the thieves.

The con artists who lifted T-Data's identity did the same thing with dozens of other small companies, including a long-term health care management firm and some other technology businesses, and apparently absconded with tens of thousands of dollars.

Merchant processors say that they see such corporate identity theft with some regularity. The criminals who ran the T-Data scam employed a few crafty tricks. For instance, to obtain a merchant account, they had to furnish a tax ID number. Giving the real number of T-Data might have foiled the plan. So they handed over the name and Social Security number of a man who had nothing to do with T-Data but who they said was the company's president. They had stolen his information too, and in fact he never knew that it was his sound credit that was checked to grant the fake T-Data accounts. To keep the real company from finding out about the scam, the thieves provided an address slightly different from T-Data's real address, hoping that any mail regarding the credit card payments would go undelivered.

What tripped the scheme up was an unlikely event. A mailman who knew the T-Data name went ahead and did deliver some of the mail to the company, despite the wrong address, and the suspicious owner called the authorities.

The New Way to Abuse Your Spouse

A lot of divorces are anything but amicable, and acts of vengeance are all too commonplace. Spouses are well acquainted with each other's key personal data, not only Social Security numbers but often passwords to accounts and credit card numbers. So an unremarked-upon application of identity theft is domestic abuse.

The interesting thing is, ex-spouses don't so much steal from each other, which can be awfully obvious. Rather, bitter divorcees or separated spouses order pornography in their spouse's name, or have merchandise they didn't purchase delivered to them. In these instances, the perpetrators are not looking to make any money—they just want to wreak havoc in the lives of their ex-lovers out of spite.

One ex-wife, privy to all her husband's passwords, tailed him through his cell phone records and tracked down other women he was seeing. Then she ordered gifts in his name and sent them to these women, deliberately putting incorrect names on them—sending flowers to Janet, say, that were addressed to Sara—to try to break up the relationships.

Money usually isn't involved in these cases, so if the victim calls the police, what are they going to do? They'll ask if the spouse physically harmed you. No. Did he or she steal anything? No. Do you have proof that your ex is behind this? Not exactly.

Abuse can even involve someone with whom you have had a neighborhood spat who doesn't know how to give up a grudge. That's what happened to one man and his wife. A neighbor from a community that they had moved out of managed to get hold of the couple's personal information. He sent it out around the country as a mock credit report and urged the recipients to make use of it. Well, guess what—many did. They went ahead and applied for a flurry of loans that the victims had to cancel. The crook put the wife's name and address on advertised pen-pal lists for prison inmates. In short order, she found herself receiving eight or nine impassioned letters a day from prisoners, many of which were downright vulgar. The crook, who apparently had far too much time on his hands, would even pretend he was the wife in online sex chat rooms. The aggravation and stress that the couple felt was overwhelming.

The versatile evils of identity theft can penetrate into every corner of daily life.

Your Identity Is Like Fine Wine

Patience is a virtue few people attribute to thieves, but the wily ones have it in abundance. That's why one of the things identity thieves do with your information is nothing at all.

Citibank got an enormous amount of unwanted publicity in 2005 when it came out that two of its computer disks had gone missing from a UPS truck. What was the big deal? Well, the disks contained unencrypted information on two million customers, so it earned a lot of press. The bank insisted that the disks were just missing, but they were undoubtedly stolen. Packages, no matter how small, don't very easily get lost by UPS. With its tracking abilities, it would have found the disks. To this day nobody knows for sure what happened to the disks, but I've got a good idea. I'll bet a criminal ring paid off a UPS person to hand them over.

Weeks after the episode, Citibank tried to reassure the affected customers (not to mention the millions of other customers who had to wonder if they were next) that no signs of criminal activity had shown up in the identities of the two million people. Well, I was amazed to hear them say that, and I said as much when I was interviewed on CNN's *NewsNight with Aaron Brown* about the caper. Identity thieves would have to be stupid to do anything with the information now, when the heat is on. That's not how the sophisticated ones work.

I'll wager you that those two disks are sitting in a vault somewhere, aging like fine wine as identities do. The people who buy that information just sell it again and again. Each time they sell it, it goes up in value. If the thieves had merely stolen credit card numbers, the victims would have canceled the cards (though not until they were actually compromised, because it costs an issuer $10 to cancel and reissue a new card, and when there are two million of them, it's not chump change and the company's not going to spend the money if it doesn't have to). But five years from now, ten years from now, you'll still have the same date of birth, you'll still have the same Social Security number, and you'll still have the same name. You can't cancel your date of birth. You can't cancel your Social Security number. You can't cancel your name.

What the thieves will do is wait five or ten years and then start stealing money in those names, when everyone's guard is down and when the potential of a lot of those names is appreciably greater. Say they picked up the name of someone in his twenties when he's still in college. Maybe he's at Wharton or the Kellogg School, working on his MBA. Why not wait ten years until he's really established, engaged in investment banking at Goldman Sachs or American Express, pulling down a nice six-figure salary with a credit rating of 780? He's got a mortgage, a car, and some money in the bank. He's ripe to have his identity assumed.

Ten years later, when that investment banker finds out his credit has been stolen, he won't even think of Citibank. He'll tell his wife, "It must have happened last week when I filled out that credit application at Waldbaum's." He'll have no idea that it happened a decade ago, when two disks vanished from a UPS truck.

You may doubt that a thief is going to leave identities gathering dust in a safe, making him no immediate money, but these identity theft rings can afford to do so because they've become veritable corporations. They've got data on people flowing in all the time, so they can easily allow information to sit idle while it grows in value. Just like a corporation, they've got inventory, and the way they manage it is, First in, last out.

A recent study by ID Analytics came to the perplexing conclusion that there's not all that much to worry about with data heists. Since it takes about five minutes to fill out a credit application, it reasoned, a thief would need to devote six and a half hours a day, five days a week, fifty weeks a year, for more than fifty years to make use of a file containing a million consumer identities. The implication was, who in his right mind would do that? Well, that's awfully naïve thinking. First of all, it's never one person but an entire enterprise that deploys these identities. Second, the enterprise intends to use them over a period of years. Third, they're going to sell a lot of those names.

Which isn't hard to do. There are numerous identity theft chat rooms where crooks sell and swap stolen information. If you go into one of them, you will often find anywhere from a hundred to five hundred people actively vying for identities. Varying packages come up for bid. You can buy a name and a Social Security number or else opt for a banking card with a PIN number. An especially choice piece of merchandise is what's called a gold profile, a profile that contains all the goods on someone: first name, last name, address, phone,

Social Security number, e-mail address, eBay account, mother's maiden name. In other words, you can buy a fully assembled crime, gift-wrapped and ready to produce money.

So if a team of thieves rounds up a million identities, some will get used, some will get sold, and many will sit quietly inactive, ripening until the right moment arrives.

6

The Twenty Steps to Prevent Identity Theft

Since punishment for identity theft and recovery of stolen funds are so rare, the only viable course of action is prevention. Now that you know how sinister identity theft can be, and that it can come at you from all sides, you might wonder if you have any chance of staving it off. You do. Nothing is foolproof against crime, certainly, and you have to be a fool to believe that anything is. But you can play the odds. Identity thieves—the professionals, at least—spend all their time trying to outwit you so they can steal your money, while you spend at most a small portion of your time trying to keep them from getting it. So the odds distinctly favor them. But you can reduce those percentages significantly if you take a number of fairly simple precautions.

My many years spent observing this crime have convinced me that the following are the twenty crucial steps that can best keep you from becoming one of its victims.

1. Check Your Credit Report

When people ask me for the number-one way to prevent having one's identity stolen, I don't even hesitate. My answer is to monitor your credit regularly. Keeping abreast of your credit history is the consumer's best self-protecting technique by far. It's so important that I'm going to devote the next chapter to the credit bureaus and credit reports.

Even if you've never had any inkling of trouble with your credit, this step is absolutely vital, whether you make $10,000 a year or $10 million. If an identity thief uses your Social Security number and name to open a new credit card account with a fake address and phone number, you may not find out about it until the damage is long done—unless you check your credit report periodically.

If you have children, make sure you watch out for fishy activity with their credit too, even if you know they have none. One young man, all of three years old, received his first letter ever from a county prosecutor notifying him that his identity had been stolen.

Years ago, when I started to think about protection against identity theft, I helped develop a program known as PrivacyGuard. All of the nation's largest banks today—Bank of America, Wells Fargo, Citibank, Key Bank, J.P. Morgan Chase, U.S. Bank—use PrivacyGuard and make it available to their customers. When I worked with what is now called the Affinion Group to design the program in 1995, I never dreamed that ten years later more than 7 million people would be using it.

All I said in 1995 was that to avoid becoming a victim of identity theft, you have to monitor all three credit bureaus—Equifax, Experian, and TransUnion. Not one, but all three. And you have to monitor them twenty-four hours a day, seven days a week. Any request for my credit would have to go through one of those bureaus. If I could be notified in real time of that happening, then I could prevent this crime from occurring. Services popped up and said they could monitor one's credit, but they monitored only one bureau. They would notify you by letter, so that meant you would know maybe five days after the fact. Or they would be in touch once a quarter, giving you an activity report. That's a little late.

With PrivacyGuard, members can request unlimited copies of their entire credit report from all three credit-reporting agencies. You receive the entire report from each bureau. You also receive your credit scores—all three of them. They may not always be the same. Suppose I'm 750 on Experian, 730 on Equifax, and 620 on TransUnion. I will wonder what's going on with TransUnion and check it out further.

PrivacyGuard also offers easy access to your driving and medical records, so you can check them for accuracy and see which companies have asked to see them. It provides up to $10,000 in identity theft insurance to help cover the costs of restoring your identity after the first $100, including legal fees, lost wages, and long-distance charges. (Don't get too worked up about this; I'll tell you about insurance at the end of this chapter.) More important, it affords professional fraud resolution assistance that helps make recovering your identity as quick and easy as possible.

PrivacyGuard costs about $12 a month. If somebody walks into Best Buy store number 1158 in Oklahoma City and applies for credit in your name to get a big-screen TV on quick credit, PrivacyGuard will notify you within 24 hours and will soon be able to alert you instantly by text message. It will give you the phone number of the store and the credit manager's name. So you call and tell the credit manager that he'd better call the police, because the person who wants that big-screen TV is not you. If you're notified about an act of theft, you can be proactive and do something about it.

I receive no royalties from this product, though I am a paid spokesperson for it. And I still use it as a member. PrivacyGuard has a lot of variations. If you go to PrivacyGuard.com and click on PrivacyGuard/Frank, you'll come to the version that I personally use to protect myself and that I recommend you use.

2. Don't Give Out Your SSN

Just because a form contains a space for your Social Security number doesn't mean you have to fill it in. Just because someone asks you for it doesn't mean you have to give it. Your payroll department may need it, but the guy on the street taking a poll about the new Brad Pitt movie doesn't. Your bank may need your Social Security number, but your grocery store's savings club doesn't. What are they going to do, run a credit check before you buy a box of Froot Loops or some bananas?

One man was filling out an application to be the coach of his son's neighborhood football team. It asked for his Social Security number and driver's license number. He realized this was crazy. All they really needed to know was whether he could get the players pumped up and devise effective game plans.

After-school sports programs frequently want copies of children's Social Security cards for the students to participate—again, an utterly senseless requirement.

A good rule to adhere to is, the less information you give out, the better. When a vendor requests supporting documentation to put on your check, don't use your Social Security number. The same holds true for your phone number and date of birth. Use something like a credit card or driver's license number, as long as that isn't your Social Security number. Do the same with résumés. A prospective employer will obviously need your phone number, but he has no need for your Social Security number or date of birth until he hires you. Thieves, in fact, place help-wanted ads in the paper, inviting résumés that are to include Social Security numbers.

A few places have the authority to demand your Social Security number—your employer, motor vehicle departments, welfare departments, and tax departments, as well as institutions that you deal with that handle transactions that involve taxes, like your bank and brokerage house. Everyone else can ask you for it, but you can say no. Even doctors have no legal authority to ask for it. Some businesses— health insurance companies, for instance—may not be willing to give you an alternate number, but it can't hurt to ask. For many years a number of states have used Social Security numbers as driver's license numbers. Only in the last few years did my state, Oklahoma, allow people to opt out of that practice. The federal government finally wised up, and under a provision of the Intelligence Reform and Terrorism Prevention Act, which took effect in December 2005, all newly issued driver's licenses can no longer contain Social Security numbers. But millions of people with licenses that don't expire for years to come still have to watch out.

Many companies use Social Security numbers as identification numbers and even put them on employee ID cards that they expect workers to wear. They don't want to change the system, because they don't want to spend the money. Well, you should insist. If you're in school, whether it's high school or college, don't let your Social Security number be your student identification number. It's a widespread practice, but it doesn't have to be. One student refused to go along and so was given an alternate, 000-00-0000. That'll do.

When a business asks for your Social Security number, ask them why they need it, what they plan to do with it, and how they'll keep it safe. It's your number, and so you have the right to know.

3. Protect Your Computer

Now that the laptop computer has become the most valuable tool in the thief's arsenal, you have to do everything possible to protect your computer from the many dark alleyways of the Web.

Not every virus lurking about your hard drive is in search of your Social Security number, and not every piece of spam you receive is a solicitation from an identity thief. But many of them are, and so you need to do several things as a defense against malicious hacking and cybertheft.

If you're using a wireless connection to access the Internet, make sure it's secure. Often people choose an insecure one to get a stronger signal. Security is more important than signal strength. Use an encrypted service. A well-constructed virus can keep track of every keystroke a person makes, which often includes passwords and credit card numbers. These malevolent programs then send the captured information back to a cyberthief. Virus protection programs search out and destroy these sneaky bits of code, and they're a must to have. But the antivirus software has to know what it's looking for. For this reason, it's vital to update your virus protection regularly.

Despite its many useful capabilities, Windows contains several well-known security loopholes that hackers often exploit for their own gain. Fortunately, Microsoft is always working to come up with security patches to stop hackers and thieves. Install the vendor-supplied software patches as quickly as they arrive.

When you venture out for a stroll in cyberspace, you use your Internet browser as your front door. Many people often overlook the fact that there are thousands of other doors, windows, and ventilation shafts—technically called ports—through which your computer can be accessed. If you leave any of those ports open, you're begging cyberthieves to come in and pirate information. Install an adequate firewall to lock these extra doors and windows.

Suppose you're surfing the Internet, and a window pops up. You don't really read it, but you click yes to make it go away. Congratulations! You just downloaded a program. It may, of course, be a friendly, harmless program. Then again it may also be a mean, sneaky program that changes your firewall settings and snoops around your computer for proprietary information. Many of these programs, commonly known as spyware, perform useful functions while also doing less desirable things just under your radar. The point is that you really don't know what these transparent programs are doing. Once you invite a spyware program onto your computer, however, it can do just about anything, and its movements can be very hard to detect.

The solution? Click no instead of yes. Your Internet browser, if properly configured, will ask you if you want to accept a download, so read those boring gray boxes carefully and choose your downloads wisely. Be wary of clicking yes to download free contests, particularly at porn, gambling, music, or game sites. Assume that any e-mail that asks you for your personal information is a fraud. If you've downloaded a lot of free software and can't seem to make it go away, you may want to invest in spy-killer or ad-killer software, which is designed to find and delete most known spyware applications.

Rather than click on links, it's always best to type in an Internet address from scratch. Double-check and triple-check that you typed it correctly. Identity thieves thrive on common typing errors. They set up addresses that are one letter off the real thing or that use frequently transposed letters—Merill Lynch rather than Merrill Lynch, say, or Chsae rather than Chase. Check any bank or brokerage Web address against your monthly statement. The same goes for the phone number.

Suspicious of a domain site or pharming? Besides the domain name—such as www.amazon.com—a website has a numeric IP address. You can go to www.networksolutions.com and click on the WHOIS tab. Type in a domain name, then search for the IP address. Type that in instead of the domain name to go to the website.

When you happen on a false or questionable Web address, tell the real bank or company about it. Customer notifications are one of the principal ways that real institutions unmask copycat sites so that they can take the necessary steps to shut them down. At the same time, if you've got good reason to think a site is fraudulent, report it to the Internet Crime Complaint Center (www.ic3.gov), a union between the FBI and the National White Collar Crime Center.

Who's the most likely member of your family to download free software—namely, music and the latest bizarre games—and infect your computer with spyware and Trojan horses? Your child. You can try to teach your kids to show restraint, but you'll have more success and less aggravation if you have them use a separate computer, not the one you use to do online banking and store your financial records.

4. Keep Track of Your Billing Cycles

It would be nice if it were true, but a missing bill doesn't mean that a credit card company or a mortgage holder is giving you a month off. Rather, it may mean that a thief has changed your address. I'm not an overly paranoid person, but I know what time of the month my American Express bill comes, when the electric bill comes, and when my car note comes due. After all, I pay them every month. I don't think you need to keep a list, but if you know the MasterCard bill usually comes on the fifteenth and now it's the twenty-seventh, then something's up. Call and figure out why they don't want your money.

I tend to pay bills when they come in. Not everyone does it that way. A lot of people keep a bill file where they accumulate the month's bills, then tackle them in one swoop or in batches. Such people may not be as tuned in. You may have so many monthly bills that it's hard to sort them out in your mind. It wouldn't hurt to be more organized and perhaps to keep a little list of what bills you're expecting and to check them off when they arrive.

The best thing to do is to try to pay your bills soon after they come in, because then you'll have a billing cycle ingrained in your mind and you'll notice when something is missing.

5. Examine Your Financial Statements like an Obsessed Accountant

As soon as a credit card statement arrives, get out your green eyeshade and go over it carefully to make sure you really bought all that stuff. If you didn't, deal with it right away. (If you did, give yourself a moment to recover from the shock—I really bought all that stuff?)

Many consumers can't bear to open their credit card bills until the last minute, when the payment must be made, and then they'll sneak a quick look at the unfortunate total and pay the amount that appears in the minimum payment box. They know they spend too much, and so no total seems too high. Well, if you don't examine every charge, you may end up paying for someone else's lifestyle in addition to your own.

You may also find mistakes. You returned that pink sweater, and yet the charge is still there. It happens more often than you think.

You absolutely must check and reconcile your bank statement each month to root out errors or fraud. Too many Americans can't be bothered, and criminals profit from that indifference. A lot of people don't even open their bank statements. They don't realize that they must notify their bank of any error or fraud within a limited period of time. After that notification period ends, the customer can be stuck with the loss.

Let's say I obtain one of your blank checks. I fill it out for $2,000, sign your name, and cash it. Let's also say you never look at your bank statement until there's a problem. Two months later you receive an overdraft notice, and you think, "That's impossible. I've got $2,000 in my checking account!" But the bank says, "Oh no, you're overdrawn." So you open your statement from two months ago and find the forged check for $2,000. The signature isn't even close to yours. But the bank may not credit you for the $2,000 because you did not report the fraud within the time allowed. Too many people don't learn about this policy until they lose money.

6. Guard Your Mail from Theft

Make a practice of picking up your mail as soon as possible after it is delivered, lest some well-intentioned thief concludes you won't mind if he takes it. Consider investing in a locked mailbox, or if you live in a particularly high-crime area, play it extra safe with a post office box.

Burn some extra calories by taking your outgoing mail to a drop box rather than leaving it in the mailbox in front of your home—the red flag up alerts thieves to come and get it. It's best to mail bill payments and other financial transactions from a post office mailbox. When you order new checks, go get them yourself from the bank instead of having them mailed.

Finally, if you go on vacation, ask a neighbor to pick up your mail, or call the post office and ask them to have your mail held for you. Best of all, put a hold on your mail and also ask a neighbor to check if any comes. A California man went away on vacation for two weeks and had the post office hold his mail. Alas, a substitute carrier, unaware of the hold order, saw the pile of mail lying around and delivered it. A thief then stole it.

Complain to your credit card company when it sends you those unsolicited free checks to entice you to transfer another card's balance. (If it's not sending you checks separately, it's often attaching one to your monthly statements.) Many credit card companies are their own worst enemies and simply consider check fraud to be part of doing business—big business. Thieves know this and make a nice living swiping those checks that you don't even know were sent until you see that $1,200 computer charge on your next statement.

7. Invest in a Shredder

These days a shredder is a must-have machine in every home. In my opinion, it's more important than the coffeemaker or the dishwasher. Get into the habit of shredding all documents before you toss them in the garbage. This goes for all bills and papers that contain personal information, especially Social Security numbers and financial account numbers. And it certainly goes for those preapproved credit card and loan offerings.

Why shred them? Because not everything you toss out ends up in the landfill with the crows. Would you put an ad in the newspaper containing your bank account number and your Social Security number? Tossing statements in the garbage with that information can have consequences just as serious.

Don't get just any shredder. Don't get a straight "spaghetti" shredder that cuts paper into straight strips. If a crook steals the garbage, he can just put the paper back together and read it. I can put the front page of the *Wall Street Journal* through a shredder and reassemble it so that I can read it within five minutes. Many of the documents in the Enron scandal were pieced back together after being shredded with vertical shredders that only ripped them into long strips.

What most people don't realize is that even the scraps from a crosscut shredder can be patched together by a highly determined crook, though it's a time-consuming endeavor. A better alternative is a crosscut shredder that reduces the paper to confetti. And it's usually the same price.

Your best bet is a shredder I've designed—it's got my name on it—called the Security Micro Cut. Unlike most other machines, it's silent and it chops up CDs, DVDs, computer disks, and credit cards, as well as paper, into unrecognizable pieces so tiny that not even a magician could patch them back together. People store a lot of personal and business information on disks, and then when they don't need them anymore, they just throw them away. These must be shredded too, along with expired and unused credit cards. Simply cutting them in half with scissors is not sufficient to foil a thief.

My multifunction shredder costs about the same as a good crosscut shredder and is sold exclusively at Staples. It comes in a home model and a heavy-duty version for office use.

People replace computers with great regularity these days, and their hard drives are crowded with tax returns and bank statements and who knows what else. A woman dumped her old computer on the curb for the garbage collector. It contained years of business records. And yes, a thief beat the trash man to it and her identity was stolen. Roughly one in twelve computers in use worldwide are secondhand machines, and at any given time thousands of used computers are up for sale on Internet auction sites. Guess who buys some of them?

If you're going to sell or discard your computer, wipe the hard drive. Either have a professional totally overwrite the drive, or buy software that enables you to do it yourself. It's best to overwrite data, because deleted files can be recovered with certain software. Programs like Eraser (free at www.heidi.ie), Sure Delete, and WipeDrive can accomplish this task. If you use a service, you have to be careful. Did you go to the cheapest one in the phone book? Did they really erase it, or did they copy it or sell it?

Some people who throw away a computer figure they don't have to bother to erase anything. They simply take a sledgehammer to it. Well, I know the FBI is pretty good at retrieving information from mangled computers, so I'm sure criminals are as well. The best solution is to do both: erase the data yourself and then remove the hard drive from the computer and physically destroy it, either with a hammer or by incinerating it.

8. Practice Safe Shopping

Ah, Internet shopping. No lines, no crowded parking lots, and you can remain anonymous. And so can the identity thief as he hacks into a Web merchant's database and steals your credit card number. To guard against Internet shopping scams, follow these simple safeguards.

Shop only from secure sites that will encrypt your order information and your credit card number before sending them to a merchant. To make sure your connection is secure, look for *https://* at the beginning of the URL in the address bar. It's the *s* that's important. Also check for a little picture of a padlock or an unbroken key in the bottom right-hand corner of your browser window.

Use only one credit card for all online purchases. That way it's easier to keep track of fraudulent charges. But if you're shopping on a department store's website and you have their credit card, then use that instead.

Shop at sites you know. If you're not sure about a site, do a little research before you divulge your private information.

Look for privacy seals like BBBOnLine, TRUSTe, or VeriSign on the sites where you shop. These colorful little logos, usually located at the bottom of a homepage, certify that the company adheres to certain privacy and security guidelines. Click on the seal to make sure it's genuine and to find out exactly what its placement on the site means.

Keep detailed records of your online purchases in case anything goes wrong.

Log off after using any public Internet terminals, and better yet, save your shopping for your home computer.

Likewise, don't make sensitive phone calls—the ones where you recite your credit card number—where other people can overhear you.

9. Avoid Sketchy ATMs

All ATMs may look pretty much alike, but I assure you they're not. Some of them are set up to copy your bank card as well as give you money. Some ATMs look like someone just put them there. Be skeptical of portable machines that you see in delis and hotel lobbies, especially ones that have a cord protruding from the back that's not plugged in. That means the data isn't being sent anywhere—it's just being recorded for a crook's eyes. You should never use an ATM that has a blank screen message that you've never seen before.

I personally stick with real, secure bank ATMs. The ones you see in drugstores, gas stations, and hotels are private ATMs that make money off the fees. Is the guy who put them there legitimate? Is he extracting the numbers off your card? These ATMs are unregulated and have been the source of giant identity theft rings. Though industry guidelines specify who should be allowed to buy an ATM, some vendors will sell to anyone who has the cash.

Mind your own business, and make sure no one else does. Keep an eye peeled for anyone standing nearby who seems a little too interested in your ATM activity. Use your free hand to shield the keypad when you enter your PIN.

10. Be Suspicious of Unexpected Calls or Letters

When a business calls or e-mails you and asks for personal information, indulge in a little healthy paranoia. It's usually a clue that something's wrong. No legitimate bank or financial operation works that way, especially in this day of heightened privacy concerns. Make it a rigid policy not to get personal unless you're the one who initiated the contact.

Even if the caller seems for real, it's best to double-check. Anyone can sound professional over the phone, and anyone can create an official-looking e-mail.

I encountered a situation recently that I immediately recognized as a scam. It started when I got an e-mail saying, "Please call this eight-hundred number concerning your MasterCard. We want to verify some recent charges. If we do not hear from you in forty-eight hours, we will have to deactivate your card." It doesn't say what kind of MasterCard, but most people have a MasterCard of some kind, so your instinct is to call the 800 number. Somebody on the other end answers, "Hello, MasterCard."

You explain about the e-mail, and the person responds, "The first thing we need to do is verify that you are who you say you are, so can I have your credit card number? Expiration date? Birth date? Social Security number?" If you oblige, they respond, "We were just checking. Have you made some recent charges in the last month?" You acknowledge that you've been using your card. "Okay, that's all," the person says. "We just wanted to verify that for your security." They hang up and immediately start using that information to morph into your identity.

What you have to do is ask specific questions. They're saying they need to verify who you are; well, you also need to verify who they are. So say to the person, "Why are you asking me for this information? You wrote to me. Just saying that you're verifying some charges is too vague. Give me a list of the charges, and I'll verify them." The con artist will usually say, as he did in my case, "Uh, okay, you don't have to give us that information. I'll just take care of it," and he hung up.

Another pretty slick scam is when someone calls and says he's from the security and fraud department at Visa. He gives a badge number: 16480. He says your card has been flagged for unusual activity: Did you buy an Anti-Telemarketing Device for $497.99? When you tell the caller no, he says, "We'll issue a credit and start a fraud investigation. If you have any questions, call the eight-hundred number on the back of your card and ask for security. You'll need to refer to this control number." He gives you a six-digit number. Before hanging up, he says, "I just need to verify you are in possession of your card." He asks you to turn it over and read the last three numbers, which are the security numbers you generally need to make an Internet purchase. Then he's done. Notice that you actually said hardly anything. He never asked for your card number. He already had that. What he wanted was that security code so he could make Internet purchases.

One of my biggest concerns is that many young people are targets of identity theft. When my three sons were at college, they often got phone calls at seven-thirty in the morning from supposedly legitimate marketers inviting them to apply for credit cards. Some no doubt were legitimate; others surely were crooks getting an early start on their criminal day. They also got swarms of mail solicitations. My kids have been trained to pass those letters on to me, but other gullible teenagers recklessly give out their information and get burned. Warn your children to keep personal information to themselves and to keep their checkbooks someplace safe. Even a roommate could be an identity thief in the making.

11. Put Real Passwords on Your Accounts

These days everyone seems to need two or three dozen passwords—for their bank accounts, ATM, brokerage account, e-mail, cell phone, work computer, home computer, and so forth. It's becoming a real hassle to keep track of them. So many people rely on short and simple combinations. Crooks count on that happening. Keep in mind that even the densest criminal will eventually crack "1234." Trust me, your pet's name is not a government secret.

You should scrupulously avoid these sorts of passwords: your Social Security number, the last four digits of your Social Security number, your mother's maiden name, your name, your birth date, your pet's name, consecutive numbers, and the word *password.* As of a year ago, believe it or not, the most common password used by banking customers was their Social Security number. Institutions, in fact, sometimes insist that you use it, either alone or in conjunction with another password, to get to your account.

I asked a friend of mine how often he checked his 401(k) balance. "Oh, pretty much every week. I'm a real fanatic," he said. How do you access it? I asked. "I call up my brokerage house, and when the automated menu comes on, I just say or enter my Social Security number." I asked if anyone was around when he did it. "Well, sure," he said. "I do it at work or on the street over my cell phone. There're plenty of people around." I think you get the point.

The smart thing to do is not to have fifteen different passwords, but to come up with one password that you can use in multiple applications that no one else will know. And never write it down. I know someone who keeps his roster of passwords at work grouped together in his Rolodex under *P* for "passwords." A strong password is a random eight-character combination of numbers, letters, and symbols. Better yet, pick something familiar to you but that only you will know. It's not related to your birthday, or a relative's name, or a pet's name, or the street you live on. Then you can adapt that password to different purposes by using that name plus 1, that name plus 2, and so on.

I rely on a password that no one could know or guess. Years ago my wife and I visited a park, and I use the park's name as my password. Some applications require a mixture of characters and numbers, so I use that name plus 1.

And don't let your browser remember your password. Never check the yes box when it asks you to remember the password for a site, and don't fill out or enable the AutoFill option.

12. Keep Your Credit Card Close When Shopping or Eating Out

When you're out spending money, watch how salespeople and waiters handle your cards—make sure they don't have a chance to copy them. Be especially alert at a store and restaurant that you've never been to before. And don't think that because you're shopping or eating at an expensive place with rave reviews, the sales help can't possibly be skimming cards. Those are just the sort of places that identity thieves try to infiltrate. They want the big spenders with big credit, not the patrons of the greasy spoon or the Dollar Store.

I was having dinner with my wife at a restaurant in London, and when it came time to pay, I gave the waiter my credit card. While he was standing next to me at the table, he swiped it with one of those handheld machines that a lot of places use to speed things up. The waiter's device sends a signal transmitting the transaction information to a register up front or elsewhere in the restaurant; you sign the screen of the device, and a receipt gets printed out. I noticed a man sitting a couple of tables away with a portable computer in his lap. He could have been using a wireless to pick up the signal from that machine and then read my credit card right on his screen. The information isn't encrypted. It's been done.

13. Use Safe Checks, and Use Them Sparingly

Make it a habit to always get your checks from your bank, because banks are far more likely to use ones that contain fraud protection features (many of which I've designed). I'm talking about things like a watermark, thermochromatic ink, chemically reactive paper, and light-sensitive ink and fibers. You may save a few bucks going with one of those check supply places that advertise in the paper, but you're putting yourself at much greater peril.

Best of all, write as few checks as you can get away with. Use a credit card instead. In today's environment they're safer and leave you less vulnerable to losses. This is an odd thing for me to be saying, because I've always been a big proponent of checks, and so I'll go into my reasoning in greater depth in Chapter 9.

Avoid debit cards as well. They're as bad as checks, since the money is instantly withdrawn from your account, and depending on the circumstances, you may be liable. With credit card fraud, the thief steals the bank's money, and your job is to prove that you don't really owe it. With debit card fraud, the thief steals your money, and you have to convince the bank to put it back into your account. Guess which one is easier? Two baggage screeners at JFK airport in New York swiped the debit card from the checked luggage of a retired firefighter headed to Miami to help victims of Hurricane Wilma. While he was down there doing good deeds, the screeners ran up charges of $3,200.

The other day I got a call from one of my sons to tell me about a friend whose debit card number had been lifted. His debit card was still in his wallet, but someone managed to obtain the number and withdraw $2,000 from his checking account. This is a young man who doesn't have much money and works very hard for what he has. When he called the bank that issued the card to report the loss, the representative asked him one question: "Does anyone have access to the card besides you?" He said, "Well, my girlfriend lives with me, but she doesn't use the card." Then the bank representative said, "But she'd be able to see the number if she wanted to, wouldn't she?" My son's friend said, "I guess if my wallet was on my dresser and she went through my things, she might see it, but she doesn't have my permission to use it."

Sorry, the bank said, claim denied due to access. See, these banks know exactly how to ask the questions so they can escape liability. My son's friend was just being honest, and the bank comes away trying to finger his girlfriend for something she didn't do.

It later turned out that my son's friend had used his debit card at a local merchant, whose software stored his account and PIN. An employee stole the information, and fake cards were created and used to withdraw money from ATMs. Once this finally came out, the bank reimbursed the young man's account.

14. Secure the Home Front and Office Front
Digging a moat around your house is probably overkill, so start small by finding a nonobvious location in your home where you can store your Social Security card, passport, and all records, including credit

card statements and tax forms, that contain personal information. You don't have to put them in a floor safe beneath the Oriental rug or even in a safe deposit box.

But don't throw them in your desk drawer, which is the first place someone would look. Try a nonobvious drawer or a far corner of the closet. As I've pointed out, burglars today often bypass the jewels and the spare cash—the things people have traditionally stuffed in the safe—because information is far more valuable. Don't make it easy for them by having an in-box sitting on a table beside the front door marked "Bills" with the latest month's array of bills to pay. Anyone could be an identity thief: the electrician, the dishwasher repairman, or your son's best friend.

Precautions are equally in order at the office. Most people just leave their purse or briefcase lying out in the open. Safely put it away in a drawer. Let's say I'm the electrician, and you say this light isn't working, and I say okay, it'll take ten minutes, you go get some coffee. Don't leave papers out on your desk with your Social Security number or valuable information displayed on your computer screen. I know people who have to enter two or three layers of passwords to get on to their computer, then leave it on all the time, including overnight.

Look into workplace security for your information. Does the guy who delivers lunch have access to your W-2, because the payroll department negligently leaves checks and financial forms out in the open? He shouldn't. Talk to your boss and explain the importance of keeping your personal information confidential.

And don't forget about the glove compartment in your car. People cram credit card receipts and spare checks in there, but they can be more desirable to a thief than your car itself. Stick with tissues and a bottle of aspirin.

15. Carry Only What You Need

Granted, it's important to be prepared, but it's no virtue to be over-prepared. Many people habitually stick their Social Security card in their wallet and carry it around with them. Why? How often, if ever, are you going to need that number during a given day? If you do, you ought to have memorized it. Leave the card at home in a secure place. Lots of people have scraps of paper in their wallet with their PIN or computer password scribbled on it, as well as other financial passwords. Some people write it all down in their daily planner that they carry around. Don't do it. Carry only the credit cards you plan to use. Don't lug your entire checkbook around with you—just the one or two checks you might write on a shopping trip.

If you lose your wallet, or someone steals it, you need to know what was in it. So make photocopies of everything, and keep them in a safe place in your home.

16. Spring Clean Your Credit Cards

If you aren't regularly using your Ham Heaven or Dollar Mania credit card, cancel it. What's the point of holding on to it, other than sentimental reasons? The more cards you have, the more opportunities a thief has to steal from you.

Do you really need twenty cards, or even five? If you have twenty, and eighteen of them you haven't used in years, are you going to notice if one has been lost? Or two of them?

I personally carry one business credit card and one personal one, and I maintain an account that only my kids use. I've never seen any reason to have more. I used to know someone who had more than fifty credit cards and liked to carry around at least two dozen of them, even though he rarely used any but his Visa and American Express. But he said it made him feel important that so many companies wanted his business, and he would brag about it. What he and most people don't realize is that having a lot of credit cards actually will lower your credit rating, so that's an additional reason not to have a sizable arsenal of them.

A lot of stores today have deals where if you apply for their card on the spot, you'll save an immediate 10 percent on what you just bought. Everyone likes to save some bucks, but don't bother with those cards. They elevate your risk of having your identity stolen, and they also lower your credit score. The salesperson will look at you as if you're a fool, but get over it and come back next week. The merchandise will probably be 10 percent lower by then anyway.

Keep it simple. And maintain organized records of all your credit cards so that, if a theft does occur, you can report it promptly and thoroughly.

17. Opt Out

I don't know about you, but I'm tired of getting those annoying calls from direct marketers just as I take my first bite of dinner. I'm equally sick of the ongoing avalanche of junk mail and spam that shows up on a daily basis. At least the mail doesn't come on Sunday, but the spam does. So get your name off of these marketing lists that get sold and resold. The reason is not to relieve the annoyance; rather, if fewer businesses have and sell your data, fewer thieves will be able to steal it.

Complain about those preapproved credit card offers too. Prescreened or preapproved offers are based on information in your credit report that indicates that you satisfy certain criteria. Believe me, you don't need those cards or the offers. Any thief can simply raid your mailbox, put another name on an offer, say that he or she has changed addresses, and—voilà—it's open season at Tiffany's with "your" card. Opt out of the offers by calling 1-888-5-OPTOUT.

And don't bother to fill out those warranty information cards that come with so many items that you buy. Your new vacuum cleaner will work regardless of whether you answer the questions.

18. Read Privacy Policies

People get privacy policies in the mail all the time, but they usually disdain them as they do the junk mail I just advised you to opt out of. But these policies are truly worth reading. I know they're dull and impossible to comprehend—that's why I'll tell you how to read them and advise you on what to look for in Chapter 8—but they're essential for understanding what your bank, financial institutions, and other businesses that you deal with do with your information. They will also tell you what restrictions you can place on the dispersal of that information. I'd recommend that you elect all the restrictions available to you.

19. Protect a Deceased Relative

When someone dies, they often move to the top of the list of identities sought after by thieves. Don't let it happen to your deceased relative. Contact the credit bureaus and have a "deceased" alert put on the person's reports. Have copies made of the relative's death certificate, and send one to every institution where the person had an account or a loan. This also goes for health insurers and the motor vehicle bureau.

As a guard against fraud, the Social Security Administration maintains what it calls a Death Master File, a massive list that houses the names of some 65 million dead people. Credit bureaus subscribe to monthly updates of the file. It can take a couple of months, however, before a name gets added to the database, and the system is imperfect enough that some names never get recorded. The normal process is for a relative or a funeral director to notify the state of a person's death, then the state tells the Social Security Administration, which adds the name to the master list. To make sure it happens, and happens quickly, inform Social Security yourself, directly, with a copy of the death certificate.

The Direct Marketing Association, the country's biggest direct marketing organization, keeps an online registry to remove dead people from its phone, direct mail, and e-mail lists for a dollar. (The cost covers confirming that the person is actually dead and verifying credit card information.) Tell them about your relative's death too.

20. Place Fraud Alerts on Your Credit Reports

Putting a *fraud alert tag* on your credit report will limit a thief's ability to open accounts in your name. New creditors will generally contact you before they grant credit, though some will refuse to be bothered. You need to call only one of the three credit bureaus to place the alert, since they're required to contact the others. Fraud alerts are free and last for ninety days. You can terminate them earlier, and you can also renew them. If you've been a victim of identity theft, you can place an extended fraud alert on your report that remains in place for seven years. These alerts will slow down your ability to get credit, but as long as you're willing to accept that slight inconvenience, give yourself all the protection that's available.

If you're a member of the military and are going off on deployment, put an *active duty alert* on your credit report. Again, this tag forces creditors to verify your identity before granting credit in your name. Of course, it may not be convenient to call you if you're fighting a war, but you're permitted to designate a personal representative to act in your stead. These alerts last one year but can be removed earlier at your request or be renewed. This action also gets you off the national marketing lists for prescreened offers from credit issuers for two years, unless you ask to be reinstated earlier. In my opinion, you don't ever want to be reinstated.

I'm convinced that following these tips will make a big difference in protecting you against identity theft. As I've said, nothing is foolproof. But if you make it hard for thieves to get your identity, then their inclination will be to leave you alone and try someone else.

Forget Insurance

Before moving on, I'd like to say a few words about a new product that has emerged and become an industry in its own right: identity theft insurance. Insurers, banks, and credit card companies have increasingly been offering this product. You can actually add it right on to your homeowner's policy. Some banks and credit card issuers provide it free, up to a certain amount, as a perk. As far as I'm concerned, the entire idea is really a scam.

You ask someone, "Do you have it?"

"Yeah, I got it for twenty-five dollars."

"What do you think it does?"

"Well, if someone steals my identity the insurance company will give me my money back."

Absolutely not. No insurance company will do that. I've read through these policies, and you have to be an attorney to figure out that you're not getting your money back. These policies are actually perverse. Having one tends to make you drop your guard because you think you're covered.

The insurance is cheap, because the losses to the victim are usually small. The real cost is loss of time, which these policies cover in a limited way. They put restrictions on how much you can claim in "lost" wages—for instance, $500 a week for four weeks. But if you're on salary, like most people, you're not out any wages, just your own time and anguish. Plus many policies have deductibles of anywhere from $100 to $500.

All the insurance does is give you an inflated sense of security that you have nothing to worry about, when actually you do. And some people end up buying coverage that is already included in their homeowners' insurance, giving them two worthless policies. *Consumer Reports,* to its credit, put identity theft insurance on its list of "10 insurance policies you don't need." The nonprofit Identity Theft Resource Center says that as far as it knows, this insurance never does any good. In 2005 it put a survey on its website asking for feedback from people who had collected claims, then finally removed it after a few months because no one had responded.

To this day, I don't understand why people have also bought policies that insure their credit cards. You see ads that for $80 a year your credit card will be protected from theft. If you have your wallet stolen, you call them up and they'll take care of everything. I say to people, you're not even liable. You have thirty days by law to notify the card issuer without being responsible for any charges. It doesn't matter if the thief charges $1 million worth of goods— you're not liable. If you don't notify them in thirty days, the most you're responsible for is $50, and often that's waived.

So I've asked these insurers, "How do you justify selling this?" And they say, "Well, you might have eleven cards and you don't notice your wallet has been missing." If my wallet was missing for thirty days, I'd notice it.

Nonetheless, millions of people have bought this insurance, and it's still being sold. It's the most absurd thing I've ever heard of. Even Affinion, for whom I serve as a spokesperson, sells it. But I've told them that some of their products I approve of, while others I think are worthless. My arrangement with them is that I will endorse only the ones that I feel work. They know that I'm not big on identity theft insurance and credit card insurance. Affinion, for instance, offers a $49-a-year version of PrivacyGuard that notifies you of a credit problem by mail. That's not good enough—a thief is acting as you, and you find out a few days later? They justify the product by saying that some people won't pay $100 or so and thus they want to offer a cheaper product for them. But it doesn't work.

That's why I don't promote it—only the product that I use, PrivacyGuard/Frank. It happens to include insurance as well, yet you're not really paying for it, because all the other services— immediate notification, unlimited access to your credit reports, and a resolution service—are worth the price alone.

So beware of fraud protection programs that sound good but are worthless. In the 1990s, for instance, some banks touted credit cards that contained a photo of the cardholder. That might sound like a worthy idea, but salespeople rarely bothered to look at the photos, and the pictures were of no use in telephone and online transactions.

A number of services have sprung up to monitor people's personal data for them and let them know if anything looks fishy. For a fee, they'll run down all the personal information on you that's in public records and floating around the Web. Some of these services not only tap into the databases of credit agencies but accumulate information from property records, post offices, and licensing boards, among countless other sources. They'll let you know if a thief has set up a false mailing address in your name to receive fraudulent credit card statements.

On the face of it, these services might seem appealing, but they pose real risks of their own. You have to give the service you hire your Social Security number and other personal data. What if a thief breaks into the database of the protection service? There goes your protection. And what, if anything, do you know about the backgrounds of the people who work at these places? So I'd be very wary, especially since anything they can do, you can do on your own. I'd rather trust myself.

7

Understanding Trade Lines
and the Meaning of R2

Not long ago one of my sons, in preparation for a job, got hold of his credit report. He was a little mystified. An American Express card was listed on the report that, according to the information, would have been obtained when he was eight years old. I've always considered him precocious, but not that precocious.

He contacted the credit bureau that compiled the report to point out the error. They told him that since the account was listed in his name, it must be his account. Common sense went out the window. Eight-year-olds, he pointed out, tend not to have American Express cards. He had to write a letter reinforcing that rather obvious point and await an inquiry. Finally the card vanished from his report. We never did determine its origin. It had been used regularly for more than a decade, and the bills were always paid on time, which is why it never came to my son's attention. It could have been a mistake. Or it could have been something more nefarious.

There was also a Discover card of more recent vintage listed that didn't belong to him. In this case, despite his best efforts, he couldn't get the credit bureau to strike it from his report. They kept saying, "It shows that you have a Discover card, you must have a Discover card." Because Discover is a client of mine, I was able to go to them and say, "Hey, you've got a mix-up here. You're listing my son as having a card, and he doesn't." They sent a note to the credit bureau confirming that fact. Had I not known someone at Discover, my son would still be living with that card. And that might have restricted how much credit he would be granted, because creditors could have concluded that he already had more than enough.

Nothing about these stories is at all unusual. In fact, if your credit reports are entirely accurate, you're a very lucky person, and a member of a distinct minority. I'm a stickler about requesting credit reports on a regular basis, then actually sitting down and reading them. As you recall, this is my number-one step to avoid identity theft, and due to its significance I want to discuss the subject in some more detail.

One of the primary reasons identity thieves are so successful is that most people don't bother to read their credit report or even know how to read one. And even those who do often fail to appreciate how important it is and how a single line buried somewhere in the dense body of their report can radically affect their future.

An Industry of Errors

Twenty years ago credit reports weren't that big a deal. But today just about everything is based on credit. This is true whether you earn $7.75 an hour or $750,000 a year. Credit reports are a financial impression of you. They determine whether you can afford big things (a house, a car, a boat, a plane) or small things (a cell phone contract or getting the electricity switched on). They determine whether you go to a certain college and whether you get a mortgage, a car loan, insurance, and a job, even whether you keep the job that you already have and may have had for thirty years. Companies today let employees go all the time because of bad credit, or what appears to be bad credit, on their credit report. This is especially true if you handle money. Brokerage houses, banks, and title companies may run a credit check every ninety days on employees who have direct access to company money. If they see that Frank Abagnale is heavily overextended on all his credit cards and perhaps has a gambling problem, they will figure that he may be ripe to engineer an embezzlement scheme. So they show him the door.

It's gotten so ridiculous that doctors and hospitals regularly check your credit, even though you're not asking them for any. Despite the fact that you've got medical insurance and are going to pay the copayment yourself in cash, they still often go ahead and examine your credit when you sign in. I always ask them, why are you running my credit report? I'm not looking for credit—I'm paying cash. They look puzzled and shrug their shoulders. They have no idea why they're doing it. It's just a reflex thing to do. Dentists sometimes do it. Veterinarians sometimes do it, and you can bet they do if Rover needs some surgery. If it gets any worse, the barber will start doing it.

As it is, something like 4.5 billion pieces of data are entered each month into credit records: bill payments, bankruptcies, court judgments, overdue child support payments, foreclosures, and liens. One reason to read your reports religiously is that much of that information is wrong. Credit bureaus make more mistakes than any industry I've ever heard of.

When the Federal Reserve inspected 250,000 credit reports in 2003, it determined that an astounding 70 percent of them contained mistakes. Some of the errors were undoubtedly innocent, but others were signs of identity theft being committed. In 2004 the U.S. Public Interest Research Group, a consumer advocacy organization, concluded from a smaller review of two hundred reports in thirty states that almost 80 percent had mistakes. Many of those mistakes were trivial, but the study found that a full quarter of all the reports had errors consequential enough to cause someone to be denied a loan or refused a credit card. Some other sobering findings: 54 percent of the reports contained personal identification information that was misspelled, long outdated, or belonged to a stranger; and 30 percent listed credit accounts that had been closed by the consumer and yet were still listed as open.

Finding those mistakes, though, is the equivalent of going on a scavenger hunt. Years ago, before consumer groups started exerting pressure on the credit bureaus, credit reports were virtually indecipherable to the layperson. You really needed a Ph.D. to read one. They've gotten a lot simpler, but they're still more complicated than they need to be. I even have difficulty with them—I'm always turning the sheet over to consult the key to see what the letters mean—and I'm used to reading them. So I'm going to explain to you how to read them. But first a word about their authors.

Ever Seen a Credit Bureau?
Everyone knows their generic name: the credit bureau. And that's pretty much where it stops. Who are credit bureaus, what are they,

and what do they do? Those are basic questions that the average con-sumer would be hard pressed to answer. Judging from the way American mailboxes are perpetually crammed with the latest batch of dazzling credit offers, people are too busy collecting credit, and then gleefully using it, to monitor their credit.

So how does a credit bureau work? Basically, credit bureaus are in the business of snooping into how quickly and reliably you pay your bills. The name *credit bureau* sounds awfully official, but these organizations are neither government agencies nor nonprofit entities. They're in it for the money. And while they're more regu-lated than they used to be, they're still pretty freewheeling opera-tions.

A number of small local credit bureaus are scattered around the country, but there are three major ones—Equifax, Experian, and TransUnion. They're the ones you need to be concerned with, since the local services tend to report their information to one or all of the big three.

Credit bureaus make their money by selling the information on people's credit reports to businesses like banks, savings and loans, fi-nance companies, credit companies, and retailers, who review the in-formation in order to decide whether to issue credit. If you think for a moment that the bureaus are working in your interest, you're mis-taken. The customers of the credit bureaus are the merchant and the bank, not you the consumer. They have an enormously important impact on your life, but they don't serve you. They serve the credi-tors, who pay them. Credit bureaus would love it if you never got to see your credit report. That's the way it used to be until fairly re-cently, when federal legislation forced them to furnish it to you free, provided that you ask for it.

What's always bothered me is that the burden is always on you. It's up to you to see that your credit is accurate. But if you don't get your report, you don't know if it's accurate. When you find something wrong on your report and you tell them, they say, "Well, that's what the merchant said. You'll have to call him." I love the game—it always puts you on the defensive.

Another thing has always bugged me. Say Frank and Sonny decide to open a molasses business in Vermont and sell molasses by mail order. So they go to the credit bureaus and say they're doing this and they need to check the credit on some customers. It gets duly handed over. I don't think the bureaus vet these merchants very well. My impression is that just about anyone can pull a credit report. A guy who has a hole-in-the-wall store in Brooklyn can pull a credit report. Maybe he's checking on whether you're good for the dishwasher you bought from him—or maybe he's selling your information to identity thieves.

They Know Everything

If you haven't taken a look at your credit report recently—or ever—you might be surprised to learn how much information credit bureaus amass about you. It includes:

✳ Your name, address, Social Security number, and employment information.

✳ The credit accounts that have been opened in your name, and the current status of those accounts, whether they're active or closed.

✳ The balance on each account, how much your monthly payments are, and whether or not you make those payments on time.

✳ Whether other companies have ordered your credit report in the past.

Where do they get all this information? Some of it, such as your name and address, is compiled from public records. The bulk of it, though, is reported to the credit bureaus by banks and other businesses that have issued you credit. These companies report to the credit bureaus on a monthly basis, telling them what your balance is and whether you've been keeping up payments. Creditors also notify the credit bureaus if you—or an identity thief posing as you—open up a new credit account. So even if there are no other clues that your identity has been stolen, your credit report can tell you if someone has been obtaining credit in your name.

When you apply for any kind of credit—a car loan, a home loan, a boat loan—the bank checks you out by ordering your credit report. Based on your credit history, the bank then decides whether to approve your loan application. Employers and landlords commonly order your credit report when weighing whether to hire you or rent you an apartment. So a lot of important developments in your life hinge in part on them.

If an identity thief has been using your identity to open bogus accounts, those actions will show up on your credit report and negatively affect your credit. And guess what? Identity thieves don't tend to pay their bills on time. In fact, they prefer not to pay them at all.

The upshot? The bank won't exactly be eager to lend you money. A company may pass you by and hire someone with better-looking numbers. So you don't need only to dress for success. You need a well-dressed credit report for success.

They Check Nothing

That the bureaus have all this influential information might not be so bad if they at least bothered to check it. But credit bureaus basically verify nothing anymore. It used to be, if you said you worked at IBM, then the credit bureau called up IBM and confirmed that you worked there. The bureau would say, "We don't need his exact salary, but is he five figures or six figures? How long has he been there?"

Now the credit bureau may not even list on your credit report where you work, because companies have stopped telling them anything, or they write down your employer based on what you say. It's part of all these laws that have come about having to do with your privacy. You might think that a law that silences your employer protects your privacy and is a good thing, but some of these laws have actually made it easier to defraud you.

But What's My Score?

Each credit bureau, after it rounds up the information on you, proceeds to calculate your credit score, a single three-digit number that summarizes your financial well-being. Your score tells lenders whether you're someone they can safely lend $10,000 to and not have to worry about getting it back or if you're one step from living in your car.

Credit scoring was invented in the 1950s by two Stanford University researchers—Bill Fair, an engineer, and Earl Isaac, a mathematician—who went on to found a company called Fair Isaac. The automated "FICO" scores that are currently widely used were introduced by the company in 1989. All three major credit-reporting agencies use variations of the Fair Isaac scoring formula under different names. The best known are the Beacon score and the Empirica score. These scores underlie billions of credit and marketing decisions each year.

Credit scores are typically calculated in a range between 300 and 850, 850 signifying lowest risk. Your score is based on such factors as whether you make payments promptly, how much credit you have, and how long you've had various accounts.

About 10 percent of Americans have a score of 800 or higher, which is excellent, while 700 is considered good. If you are below 600, you may have loans turned down or be charged much higher interest rates than those commonly advertised. You can have anything short of a truly miserable score and still get money, but you may pay dearly for it. A top FICO score—720–850—could mean a loan of 5.5 percent, while a 500–559 score could mean 9.5.

Last year the three major credit bureaus unveiled a new common scoring system, called VantageScore, that measures a consumer's credit with letter grades. The purpose is to make scores easier to comprehend for consumers and to try to eliminate some of the wide discrepancies in the scores from the different bureaus. I'm dubious, based on past experience, that vendors will quickly accept the new system and back away from the popular FICO score. Even if they do, the letter-grade approach still doesn't solve the chronic issue of all the incorrect data that undermines these scores.

It's pretty ridiculous that when the credit bureaus show you your credit report, it doesn't include your score. It is, after all, your score. They'll report it to merchants but not you. (If you take out a mortgage or loan, you can ask the loan officer for your score, and he's required by law to tell you.) There are services that you can pay to get your score, and the credit bureaus will gladly sell it to you, but I find it outrageous that the bureaus don't give it to you free along with your report. As far as I'm concerned, this is one more scam. The bureaus basically say they charge for the scores because they're entitled to. I'll bet that lobbyists for the bureaus got the legislation written so it didn't require the credit score to be included with your free report.

The report is worth a lot less without the score. There's no way that you can figure out the score yourself. People are always being told to keep good credit, are scolded when they don't, and are given tips on how to improve their credit score, and yet they have to go out of their way and pay to find out the score that they're trying to improve. They have to decide what sort of mortgage or loan to get, yet they don't have one invaluable piece of information—their credit score. It's like students taking the SAT and then trying to decide which colleges to apply to without knowing their results.

Read It Every Three Months

As I said previously, to stay on top of your credit situation and give yourself half a chance of catching identity theft soon after it happens, you need to regularly review your credit report. A lot of people will look at it occasionally, but not on a regular cycle. They think that if they inspect their report once a year, they've got things under control. But identity thieves move fast and can do a lot of damage to your credit in twelve months, so you need to look at it more often than that, probably every three or four months.

The other mistake people make is they order their report from only one agency. If life were simple, your reports from the three agencies would be identical. Life isn't simple, and chances are they aren't identical. They may be close, but they'll differ, and sometimes significantly. The bureaus may receive different information, and there's likely to be a typo or two just to keep things interesting. The reason is that credit reporting is a voluntary system. A creditor picks which agency or agencies it wants to subscribe to, and it might pick one, two, three, or even none. If I'm a jeweler, I might have an agreement with TransUnion and that's it.

When checking your creditworthiness, a lender might order your report from only one bureau. This means that a sign of trouble, like the request a bank makes when a thief applies for a car loan in your name, will appear on only one of the three reports.

In the past, to obtain your credit report you had to buy it, except in a few states or under certain exemptions. But the Fair Credit Reporting Act now requires all three nationwide bureaus to provide you with one free report every year. To simplify the process, they have established a central website, a toll-free number, and a mailing address for ordering your copies. The site is annualcreditreport.com; the number is 1-877-322-8228; and the address is Annual Credit Report Service, P.O. Box 105281, Atlanta, GA 30348-5281.

When you're on the Internet, you'll notice plenty of imposter websites that say they offer free credit reports. They actually end up enrolling you in a trial period that turns into a pay service without your being aware of what happened. And some of them are even worse—they're phishing scams designed to collect your personal information.

Besides the legally required free annual copy, you get a complimentary copy if you're unemployed and planning to apply for a job in the next sixty days, if you're on welfare, or if you've been turned down for a loan or a job because of a bad credit report and request it within sixty days. Identity theft victims also have the right to a complimentary report from each bureau.

Trying to locate on the credit bureau websites the option for those entitled to a free report because of these factors is quite a feat. A cryptic reference, in gray fine print, will be hidden at the top, bottom, or sides of the screen. You might have to pull out a magnifying glass to locate it. If you don't have an exemption, you can order your credit report more often than once a year, but you'll be charged around $10.

The best way to do things is to order your free reports once a year, but stagger the dates. Look at Equifax in January, Experian in May, and TransUnion in September. Then at no cost you're reviewing your credit every four months. Anytime you notice something unusual, immediately order the other two so that you have as much information as possible.

But What Does It Mean?

Getting your credit report is the easy part. Now comes the hard part: reading it.

Credit reports are rumored to be written in English, but they actually seem to be written in a language not yet recognized by any organized society. Don't panic. It's not necessary to take Creditese as a second language.

To find signs of identity theft, you don't have to understand every last detail of your report. Here's how to cut through the thicket.

A credit report is split up into four broad sections: Identifying Information, Credit History, Public Records, and Inquiries.

The identifying information, also called the Applicant or File

Variations section, at the beginning of the report is the boilerplate of who you are. It runs through your personal information: name, date of birth, Social Security number, current and previous addresses, phone numbers, driver's license numbers, employer, spouse's name. Your report will also list aliases and former names. Make sure that all of these are real names that you used. To simplify things and prevent errors, always use the exact same name when you are applying for credit. Make a choice now whether to incorporate a middle initial, and stick to that choice.

This opening portion is pretty straightforward, but doublecheck it anyway. It's not at all uncommon for errors to occur even here, such as different spellings of your name, multiple Social Security numbers, and other people with the same last name and different first names. If your name is Smith or Jones, you're liable to find a torrent of mistakes. But it can happen to everyone. I had my wife check her report under her maiden name, and she found a Texas woman listed whose name was similar but otherwise had no business being on her report.

You might find your date of birth given inaccurately, or an address listed where you've never lived. Someone may simply have made a mistake and reported the information wrong. But it could also be a clue that someone who isn't you has opened a credit line in your name.

The R0s and R9s

Next comes the Credit History section, and depending on how active you are, it can be rather lengthy, because it enumerates all of your credit accounts and credit behavior. It's basically your history of borrowing, reduced to names and digits.

This section is the heart of the report, and understanding it takes some effort. The accounts enumerated here are known as *trade lines*. Each trade line includes the creditor's name and the account number. Some reports will scramble the number as a safeguard, but others won't. Each account is recorded exactly the way that the merchant reported it. A line may refer to Saks Fifth Avenue, or it may be a jumble of numbers, and you have no idea what the account is. It's quite common that several accounts from a creditor will be listed; Saks may be listed four times even though you have only one account there. The explanation could be that you moved. Since you're living somewhere new, they switch your account to a different location and give you a new number, not bothering to eliminate the old number. Move three or four times, as many people do, and you'll find yourself with accounts galore. I warned you this wouldn't be easy.

Each trade line discloses when you opened the account and the nature of the credit. It may be installment credit, such as a mortgage, car loan, or education loan, which is repaid in equal monthly payments over a fixed time period. Or the credit may be revolving, such as credit card balances, department store credit, or a personal line of credit, in which there are no set number of payments but a minimum sum is due each month. Interest is assessed to any carry-over balance, and there's always a credit limit. The trade line will often run through a bunch of other basic information on the loan: the loan amount or credit limit, how much is still owed, whether the account is open or closed, how reliably you've paid the balances, and the like. Hopefully, it's all correct, but that's asking a lot of a highly imperfect system.

The credit balances always lag behind reality. You may have settled a balance forty-five days ago, but it remains stubbornly unpaid on your report because the bureaus are usually one or two months behind in posting these things. I find that unacceptable, because if you apply for credit, your current balance is what matters. Information from a credit bureau is only as accurate and timely as what creditors provide.

When you look over your report, check each trade line very closely for accounts that you don't recognize. For the accounts that are legitimately yours, make sure the number in the Balance Owing column jibes with what you've actually spent.

You'll commonly discover things like loans and mortgages listed twice, because they are sold and resold to new lenders. Or they're someone else's. A man in Massachusetts applied for a loan to do some renovations on his house. He was so sure of getting it that he started the work before the loan was formally approved. He totally ripped apart his kitchen and temporarily shoved the stove into the living room. And then the loan wasn't approved. The bank said that his credit report showed that he owed property taxes on two homes in a nearby town. But he had never lived there, let alone twice. One home belonged to another man who happened to have the same fairly common name. The other belonged to a man with an entirely different name that had mistakenly crept into his report.

Figuring out how you're doing with your debt repayment gets a bit complicated. Sometimes the report's payment history is expressed in recognizable English. It will be recorded, say, that you faithfully pay your Visa bill "always on time." On the other hand, you're told that your Macy's bill is "typically sixty days late." In other cases, the report gives the news in another tongue, using jargon like "charged off." (*Charged off* means the creditor assumes you're never going to pay and has eaten the debt.) Often the reports rely on payment codes that range from 1 to 9, and this catapults you into a new world of obfuscation. The reports will use R to stand for revolving credit and I for installment, and then grade each account. An R1 or I1 means you pay that bill within one month—in other words, on time. R2 means you pay within two months, and so on into escalating lengths of tardiness. R7 or I7 means your debts have been bunched together and are being repaid under consolidation. R8 is rather dismal news—your debt was satisfied by repossession. The worst news is an R9, which is when you've defaulted and the debt has been deemed uncollectible. R0, by the way, means you've just entered the wonderful world of credit and haven't been out there spending sufficiently for the credit wizards to judge your behavior. In other words, you're a novice just beginning to get high on borrowed money.

Some people by nature are highly consistent in their credit patterns. They're R1s or R2s with every outstanding balance. Often, though, people are inconsistent. When money is tight, they'll pay off the bills they decide are most important and let others slide. Therefore, the maze of numbers will vary markedly from line to line. You'll be an R1 with one credit card, an R5 with another, and an R3 with a third.

If a trade line is unfamiliar to you but the bill payments are up to date, don't ignore it. An identity thief may be using your name and ID to get a loan, which he is then temporarily repaying promptly so as not to attract attention. Don't make the mistake of thinking that an up-to-date account is a benefit to your credit score. You could wind up being denied credit later on when the person suddenly defaults on "your" loan—or even simply because you now have too much credit.

The Bad Stuff

The next section to the credit report is bad news if anything is listed there. This is the Public Records section. Nothing gets put here that's positive. For most people, it should be blank. It's what gets culled from court records. Arrests and criminal activities aren't included, but financial events such as bankruptcies, judgments, overdue child support, and tax liens are. A *lien* is a legal claim placed on a person's property, such as a car or a house, as security for a debt. A lien may be placed by a contractor who did work on your house or by a mechanic who repaired your car and didn't get paid. The property cannot be sold without paying the lien. Any of this nasty stuff will severely wreck your credit.

And it stays there for a good long time. Negative information remains in place for seven years. A bankruptcy stays on for ten years, even if you're no longer in bankruptcy. A note is simply posted that you've come out. And there's no time limit at all on some quirky matters like information you supplied in an application for a job that pays more than $75,000 a year.

Who's Looking

The final section, Inquiries, tells you who has requested your credit report. Potential creditors typically request it before giving you a credit card or extending a loan. But anytime anyone takes a look at your report, an inquiry gets posted. Even when you call the credit bureau and ask for a copy, your request will be listed there as an inquiry.

There are lots of different reasons why someone would want to take a peek at your credit report, but the industry sorts inquiries into two basic varieties: *hard* and *soft*. Hard inquiries are ones made because you have initiated them by applying for credit at a store or bank or for a car loan. They can come about when you arrange for a payment schedule for your kid's banjo lessons. Soft inquiries are those made without your initiation—when, say, an insurance company checks up on you because it's going to renew your policy. Or when a company wants to send out some of those junk-mail overtures to a prequalified group. Or when a creditor, for whatever reason, decides to inspect your money history. And anytime you ask to see your report, that's considered a soft inquiry.

If your report is peppered with inquiries, that can damage your credit score and impede your ability to line up fresh credit because lenders tend to be wary of people who shop excessively for loans. All too often they're maxing out credit card after credit card to sustain a debt-loaded lifestyle. To be sure, most inquiries are discounted by the scoring systems. The soft inquiries, for instance, don't appear on the reports that lenders see and are not factored into your credit score. You could have a hundred soft inquiries—or a thousand—and they won't budge your score one point. What's more, all inquiries made within thirty days of your getting a mortgage or car loan don't count. Two or more hard inquiries from mortgage or auto-loan brokers within a two-week period are tabulated as just one inquiry, a process known as *de-duplication*. The rationale is that the inquiries are for a single loan and the bureaus don't want to penalize a consumer who hunts for the best rate. And credit bureaus love it when you shop around—they're delighted if you apply to twenty banks in pursuit of the lowest rate—because every lender who pulls your credit report has to pay the bureaus a fee.

But say you go out and get a Visa card, and you charge a bunch of merchandise on it. Then three weeks later you get a solicitation from MasterCard that allows you to transfer all your debt onto its card at a lower rate. If you make the transfer, it's another inquiry. You're doing something that's financially shrewd, yet the credit bureau deducts points from your credit score.

The Inquiries section is very important, because if an identity thief got a credit account in your name, the credit card company would be listed here, on at least one of the reports. So look carefully for peculiar inquiries that you don't remember authorizing.

You Can Correct Your Credit Report

Anytime you detect something amiss in your credit report, don't dawdle or put it on your list of things to do on a slow day. Correct the discrepancies as quickly as possible. And that goes for anything that doesn't make sense, even a minor error.

The first thing to know is, it's your right to have your report corrected. The law states that both the credit bureaus and the information sources—the credit grantors who gave them the information about you—are responsible for correcting inaccuracies in your report. To make sure they really do, attack on both fronts: contact the credit bureaus as well as the information providers.

First call each of the three credit bureaus, then follow up in writing. Your letter should be detailed and specific. Identify each item you are disputing by the name of the company and the type of account. In each instance, explain the reason you are disputing it, and ask that it be corrected or deleted. Include any supporting documentation that you have, such as a police report. If you already have documents from the credit grantor agreeing that the charge or account is fraudulent, you definitely want to attach copies.

The credit bureau is allowed thirty days to investigate your case. If it deems it frivolous and decides not to bother with it, it has to let you know within five days. The credit bureau then sends you a written report on the outcome. If the information provider—the store or bank where a theft occurred—determines that your claim is legitimate and the items you are disputing are in fact incorrect, they are responsible for notifying all the credit bureaus they work with. The bureaus then must correct or delete all of the inaccurate information, including all fraudulent accounts and charges and any fraudulent inquiries.

Once you've finished, spread the word and make sure everyone knows the story. The last thing you want, now that your messed-up credit report has been cleansed of errors, is for no one but you to know about the improved outcome. If you tell them to, the credit bureaus are required to send a corrected copy of your report to any business that has received it in the last six months, as well as to any employer who has looked at it within the last two years. That's not everybody, but it's a good enough sampling to restore your good name. If there are still problems with your credit report, you can ask to have a statement added to it to explain your side of the story, which is a lot better than doing nothing.

Not all justified complaints have a happy resolution. As long as a charge is under dispute, that contested charge will show up on your report. Everything is done to make it difficult for you. If a creditor disagrees with your version, a charge could stay on forever. Suppose you bought a watch from a jeweler, and he said that you didn't pay it on time, and then the jeweler went out of business. Putting a dispute note on your report won't help; other merchants will always assume that you're wrong. After all, the other merchants who order the report are more likely to believe that their fellow merchant is right and that you're just trying to weasel out of paying a bill.

How About Those Pesky Subfiles?

Another ignoble scam of credit reports is the subfiles.

When illegal immigrants hijack your Social Security number to get a job, they may not use your name. (Often, in fact, they've bought the number and don't even know your name.) They'll just fabricate a name. And if a husky, hirsute, six-foot man from Pakistan gets a job under the Social Security number of a woman named Melody, he had better make up a name. Thus you've got two entirely different names (and sexes) attached to the same number. This sort of identity assumption is referred to as *synthetic* identity theft.

When credit information funnels into the credit bureaus under the immigrant's false name, the bureaus usually won't post it to your report because the name doesn't match (though, being mistake-prone, sometimes they will). Instead, they'll consign it to a separate file generally known as a subfile. And those subfiles aren't given to you when you request your credit report.

Well, that's great. That means that if something fishy is going on with your credit, you won't be able to find a shred of evidence of it on your own credit report. Or a synthetic thief may get a batch of credit cards and loans under your number and keep them up to date for years, setting off no alarms, until one day he defaults and every-thing crashes down on you. But you'll never know until it's too late. It's all tucked away in the subfiles.

But guess who does see those subfiles? Businesses checking up on your credit. They can also purchase a so-called Social Search from the credit bureaus that details all credit activity attached to a specific

Social Security number. But no consumer can buy one of these searches, not at any price.

So a business can see your file, plus its subfiles; decide hey, you've got an awful lot of credit; and turn you down for a loan or an apartment rental. You take a look at your credit report and can't figure out why. And that "business" that has access to your files might be nothing more than a $7.50-an-hour clerk at an apartment complex.

When the credit bureaus are pressed on this subfile issue, they get huffy and respond that they might be violating privacy rules if they let you see the credit history of someone else using your Social Security number—even though that someone else is a crook. Have we hit the height of insanity or what?

It Ought to Be Uncle Sam's Job

I wouldn't make such a big deal out of credit scores and credit reports if most consumers took them seriously, but they treat them with about as much interest as they treat nutrition labeling at McDonald's. In late 2005 the Consumer Federation of America and Providian Financial sounded a somewhat hopeful note when their survey of consumers found that 31 percent had obtained their credit reports in the last year, an improvement from 24 percent the previous year. But that still means that more than two-thirds of Americans hadn't bothered to go to the trouble of learning this critical piece of information.

Unhappily, the vast majority of consumers are muddled about what these scores are. A mere 27 percent, the study showed, understood that scores measure credit risk, not credit knowledge. Less than half realized that individuals have multiple scores, one from each of the three major credit bureaus, as well as ones from other financial institutions. Slightly more than half knew that maxing out a credit card will lower a person's credit score. (Even something as slight as an overdue library book, in fact, can reduce your score. Lots of libraries have turned to collection agencies to try to recover fines for unreturned books, and it can appear on your report under collection accounts.) Actually, less than one in four of those surveyed could even identify the three major credit bureaus. I'm not saying we've got a hopeless situation here, but a lot of work remains to be done.

What consumers have to realize is that identity theft comes at them from every direction. If flaws enter your credit report due to identity thieves that wreck your credit rating, you have been hurt not simply by the theft of money but also by the damage done to your credit standing, damage you might not even realize exists. When you go to take out a home loan and your banker tells you the rate is 8.25 percent, rather than the 7.25 percent that your next-door neighbor got, the reason might be that an identity thief has gone to town with a credit card in your name that you don't even know about.

The Consumer Federation of America and Providian determined that if people raised their credit scores by an average of just 30 points, they would save $16 billion in lower credit card finance charges alone. One simple way for many people to earn those extra points is to root out the dismal credit that has been planted on their reports by thieves.

Without a doubt, the credit report is one of the most potent documents in your life. Institutions that you rely on digest it in order to size you up. This paper means you're worthy or you're not. That's why, from my perspective, the whole concept is wrong. Here are these organizations that heavily control your life, and they're for-profit organizations. I don't think it's healthy that there are only three and that they share everything and effectively speak together. It's basically a monopoly of one. Much more of a burden should be placed on these bureaus to make sure the information they provide is accurate. In effect, they're grading you as if you were taking a test, without being sure they're looking at your answers.

Credit history should be handled by a government agency, not by a profit-making organization. That's precisely how I would organize the system if I were redoing it. That way we would no longer have businesses with their eye constantly trained on the bottom line making money off your ability to pay your bills.

8

Remember That Privacy Statement You Threw Away?

Do you know a single person who has ever read a privacy statement? I don't. Not one. These disclosures come in the mail all the time. Your bank sends them. Your brokerage house sends them. Your on-line provider sends them. Every one of your credit card issuers sends them. In fact, your own employer sends them. And each time one of the originators of these mailings makes the slightest refinement in its privacy policy, you get a fresh explanation, in elaborate, and usually stifling, detail.

The privacy statement eruption has reached the point where the average American household gets between ten and fifteen notices a year in the mail, and some lucky people receive dozens of them. On top of that, at virtually every shopping website that you visit, there's one waiting for your perusal as well.

Most people take one look at these privacy statements and dump them in the trash. I can fully sympathize. The dense print, crafted in the arcane and unfathomable language of DVD player and microwave oven instructions, persuades them that there's no point in even trying to read them. I've got a genuine interest in them, and yet even I would rather read the phone book.

It's unfortunate, because these policies are potentially extremely important, hardly in league with the deluge of unsolicited junk mail you receive from political candidates and sleazy weight-loss hucksters. They're one of the few responses that our society has made to the surge in identity theft. Since 2001, as a consequence of provisions inserted in the Gramm-Leach-Bliley Financial Services Modernization Act, every financial institution in the country, including banks, credit card companies, insurers, and brokerage houses, has been required to annually mail customers a copy of its privacy policy.

Yet it would be my guess that these notices probably rank as the least-read documents on the face of the earth. The Federal Trade Commission, which very much wants everyone to study the statements, admits that the number of people who do look at them is pathetically low. Indeed, in 2004 a federal judge threw out a collection of lawsuits against Northwest Airlines that argued that the carrier had breached its privacy policy by sharing passenger information with NASA. Why? Because the judge found that there was no evidence that any of the passengers had ever read the privacy policy.

The problem is not so much that the notices are boring, though they are. It's that they're impossible to understand, far worse than credit reports. My assumption has always been that if something is written so that I can't understand it, then the person who wrote it doesn't want me to understand it.

Well, What Is It?

The very fact that they've been sent a privacy statement leads many consumers to believe that their privacy is being safeguarded. The truth is, these statements more often are disclosures about how much of your privacy is at risk.

What exactly is a privacy policy? It essentially tells you what personal information a business collects and how it collects it. (On the Internet, companies use "cookies" as well. I'll get to them later.) It tells you how the business uses your information, who it shares it with, and what "opt out" options you have for limiting how your personal information is compiled and distributed.

By the way, if you read far enough into one of these policies to see the opt-out options, the statements then put you through so many steps to implement them that you don't do anything.

It's essential that the financial institutions, vendors, and Internet providers you patronize use your information only the way you want them to use it. But despite their outer appearances, all privacy policies are not alike, and some are basically worthless.

Calling All Scholars

Financial institutions are expert at cranking out simple, clear, and concise invitations to sign you up for yet another credit card or to urge you to take out a personal loan at a drop-dead rate. And yet these same people send out privacy notices that require the help of a high-powered microscope and a constitutional scholar to interpret. They make credit reports look like elementary school primers.

All the come-ons that make money for banks are written in big bold letters and inviting script, intentionally engineered to catch your attention. But the privacy mailings feature small, dull headlines that deliberately downplay their significance: "A statement about our privacy policy."

The law that mandates these notices explicitly states that they are to be written in a "clear and conspicuous" style, but that standard certainly isn't being met. A number of consumer opinion polls have confirmed that consumers unquestionably desire shorter and more succinct statements. In one survey, only 3 percent of the respondents said that they studied online privacy statements; the rest did not, partly because they are incomprehensible.

A couple of years ago, to assess the wordiness of privacy policies, the author of an article in *Computerworld* reviewed the online privacy statements of the Fortune Global 100 companies. This author found that American firms were the windiest, averaging 1,316 words per notice. Corporations in other countries often needed only half as many words. French companies got their messages out in an average of 723 words, while Germans came in at 690, and Dutch businesses managed with a thrifty 347.

Some policies have been getting easier to read, but they've still got a ways to go. And if U.S. companies are working to become more concise, it's been lost on me. I recently obtained the privacy statement of a prominent national company, and it came in at an exhausting 5,414 words.

How hard are the statements to understand? Well, all you have to do is read one or two to find out. Mark Hochhauser, a readability consultant who has been vocal about this issue, did an analysis in 2001 of sixty privacy notices from financial institutions and concluded that the average statement was composed at the education level of a college senior, which is eight years higher than is recommended for information intended for the general public. Some of the notices were written at the level of a graduate student. A few of the ones I've scrutinized seem designed for postdoctoral Mensa members.

Hochhauser pointed out that the notices are especially difficult for groups like the elderly and immigrants whose first language isn't English—common targets of identity thieves. Although about a quarter of adults have a college degree, he noted, studies suggest that many people read anywhere from three to five grades beneath the highest level they reached in school. That's why literacy experts suggest that documents for public consumption should be at the junior high school reading level.

Hochhauser looked into state readability requirements for other types of material that consumers might find confusing, such as insurance policies. He found that only ten of the sixty privacy notices met the insurance policy standard in Arkansas, Indiana, Kentucky, and Ohio. Three met the standard in Florida and Connecticut. None met the standard in Maine.

Some excerpts from random privacy statements that I looked at:

When a third party wants to rely on a Digital ID, it is important for the third party to know its status (for example, whether it is valid, suspended [where available] or revoked). The third party may do this by accessing our repository and querying for the status of the Digital ID. We do not generally delete Digital IDs (and their content) from our on-line repository because a third party might not then be able to check its status. You may, however, revoke (deactivate) your Digital ID. A revoked Digital ID will still appear in our repository with an indication that it has been revoked.

Got that?

How about this:

As is typical, we log http requests to our server. This means that we know the originating IP (e.g. 18.29.0.1) address of a user agent requesting a URL. We also know the Referer and User-Agent information accompanied with an HTTP request. We do not log the specific identity of visitors. We occasionally analyze the log files to determine which files are most requested and the previous site or user agent which prompted the request. Our logging is passive; we do not use technologies such as cookies to maintain any information on users. We also log requests to our search, cgi, and list maintenance services. This data is only used for administration and researching the efficacy of our tools.

Or:

With Whom Your Information is Shared ... does not share personally identifiable information with other companies, apart from those acting as our agents in providing our product(s)/service(s), and only with those partners who agree to use it only for that purpose and to keep the information secure and confidential. Also, only our parent company, entities into which our company may be merged, or entities to which any of our assets, products, sites or operations may be transferred, will be able to use personal information. We will also disclose information we maintain when required to do so by law, for example, in response to a court order or a subpoena or other legal obligation, in response to a law enforcement agency's request, or in special cases when we have reason to believe that disclosing this information is necessary to identify, contact or bring legal action against someone who may be causing injury to or interference with (either intentionally or unintentionally) our rights or property. Users should also be aware that courts of equity, such as U.S. Bankruptcy Courts, might have the authority under certain circumstances to permit personal information to be shared or transferred to third parties without permission. We may share aggregate information, which is not personally identifiable, with others. This information may include usage and demographic data, but it will not include personal information.

You can readily see why most consumers just cry uncle.

As far as I'm concerned, issuers can call these things by any flowery name that they want to, but they're really scams. The banks want to have certain information from you. An ineffective law is passed requiring them to send out these statements. The banks write them so you can't understand them. So you don't read them or do anything to restrict your information. And thus the banks manage to circumvent the law. If you're going to pass a law to protect the consumer, make it an effective one or don't pass anything.

Cookies and Whatnot

To even vaguely understand one of these statements, you need a glossary of basic private policy terms. These are the key ones:

Affiliate—A company that is owned by the company that wrote the privacy policy, or by the same parent company.

Cookie—A small text file stored on your hard drive by a website that you visit, used to identify you when you return to that site. Varying degrees of information get stored in cookies. For instance, when you go to Amazon to buy a book, the cookie allows the site to greet you by name and pull up a list of recommended books that might interest you. Some cookies are designed to remain on your computer for a long time, known as *persistent* cookies. Others are programmed to expire at a set time, called *session* cookies.

Creditworthiness—Information such as your credit score and bill-paying history that can point to the risk in giving you credit.

Joint marketer—A company that has made a deal with your company, allowing it to sell you something. For example, a company that offers financial planning might strike a deal with your bank to try to sell its service to the bank's customers. There is no law allowing you to opt out of having your information shared with joint marketers.

Nonaffiliated third party—A completely separate company, not an affiliate of your company.

Personally identifiable information (also known as nonpublic personal information)—Information that may be used to uniquely identify you, such as your name, Social Security number, credit card number, or bank account number.

Publicly available information—Things about you that anyone could find out, like your listed phone number.

Service provider (also known as agent)—A company hired by your company to perform a specific function, such as shipping or billing.

Transaction and experience information—The details about where you spend your money, such as the things listed on your credit card statement.

Do They Have Pit Bulls?

Armed with this vocabulary list, what should you look for in a privacy statement?

A good policy spells out what information has been collected, why it has been collected, how it will be used, and how it is protected. It allows you to inspect the information—after all, it is your information—and make corrections if there are errors. It enables you to see firsthand what has been assembled about you. It should have an opt-out mechanism to stop your information from being sold to secondary sources, and using that mechanism should be easy, not a chore.

You should be told the website's security system for storing your personal information, including encryption software and passwords. I worry not just about protecting information on the Web but also about the physical place it's stored. Where is the server on which it's contained? Is it in a locked room with cameras, security guards, and pit bulls? Do the guards check visitors in and out? It's very important to know the personnel policies that determine who has access to your information within the organization. How many people can see your personal information, and what background checks have been done on them?

You should be told how cookies are being used on the firm's website. Are they storing information for membership or registration purposes, or are they being used for other means? And there should be a way to opt out of tracking cookies.

In my view, you should make a practice of regularly deleting cookies from your browser, especially those from sites you no longer visit and those that contain personal information. It's easy to do. Go to Tools, Internet Options, the General tab, and there's a Delete Cookies option. That deletes all of them. You can also control how your computer uses cookies. Click the Privacy tab of the Internet options, and that allows you to set the level of cookie handling. This includes blocking all cookies. Or you can define an explicit list of sites from which you're prepared to accept cookies.

As the excerpts from privacy statements that I cited make evident, even knowing the terminology can be woefully inadequate in comprehending them. So if something isn't clear, call the company and insist that someone explain it to you in simple English. They owe it to you, because you're the customer and you're the one at risk.

Make It Opt-In

When it comes to the opt-out options contained in privacy policies, there's only one smart move to make. Use them. All of them.

Studies indicate that a minuscule percentage of consumers choose opt-out options. Estimates I've heard from banks are that less than 1 percent of customers opt out of having their information shared with other companies. I had to laugh when I read the explanation of one bank spokesperson. She said she assumed it was because customers trust their banks so much. If that's the case, then why did a 2002 poll find that nearly 80 percent of Californians were uncomfortable with financial institutions selling their information to other companies? And why did 82 percent rate the protection of financial privacy as very important, ranking it even above balancing the state budget?

I have no doubt that if people read these lawyerly privacy statements and understood their implications, most would go the opt-out route. It's crazy not to.

Regulatory tussles over whether privacy policies should offer opt-in or opt-out choices have been ongoing. Companies strongly prefer opt-out, which means that consumers have to take some sort of action to keep their information from being dispersed in ways the company wants. If the arrangement is opt-in, the burden shifts and the company has to prove that consumers granted their consent to use their information in all the ways spelled out in the policy. For the most part, businesses despise the opt-in idea, whining that it would create undue burdens and compliance costs for them that would force them to impose higher costs on consumers for their products and services.

So far, opt-out has prevailed. Some companies have implemented their own policy of not sharing consumers' information without their express permission, but they're in a distinct minority.

My view is that opt-in should be the rule—everywhere. I don't accept the woe-is-me, undue-burden argument. I don't accept that withholding information will inhibit anything worthwhile. All it inhibits is all these other companies soliciting me to buy this lawn mower or that forty-foot motor home.

The opt-out choice is itself often a challenge. It's not done in any standard way. In some instances, but not all, you get a form and a self-addressed envelope. In others, you call a toll-free number and are put through the usual automated welter of steps that are too exasperating to pursue. Some direct you to a website, while others don't. And the choice comes at the end of the notice, after all the mumbly-jumbly and propaganda. By that time you've long stopped reading. Some bank executives themselves have admitted that they have a hard time figuring out how to protect their information under their own bank's policies.

What's more, even when a consumer has gone the opt-out route for outside sharing, financial institutions can still provide the data to unrelated financial institutions under "joint marketing agreements."

The legislation governing information sharing doesn't allow

consumers to opt out of the common practice among financial institutions of exchanging basic information, known as "experience and
transaction" data, with their own subsidiaries. This data includes
things like purchasing habits, number of accounts, size of accounts,
co-account holders, frequency of deposits, and so forth. Therefore, if
you sign up with a large bank, the sort of personal information that
it collects can also find its way to the bank's brokerage and insurance
arms, whether you like it or not. Personally, I don't like it.

Big companies have a lot more of these affiliates than you probably realize. Citigroup has more than 2,700 of them. Bank of America has about 1,500. Maybe you wouldn't mind if your information
was shared with four or five affiliates. Would you mind if it was
shared with 2,700?

When the universe gets that extensive, you don't really know
who has your information. And when it gets misused, you don't
know who's misusing it. Not every affiliate necessarily has the same
security and the same privacy policy. It takes only one weak link.

What benefit is it to me if the bank I use shares my information with its brokerage arm or its insurance affiliate? I don't think
there's any benefit. If I want to do business with one of the bank's
other units, I'll do it. I don't need them soliciting me. If they want
to solicit me, let them take out an ad in the newspaper.

Another preposterous practice is that most companies don't allow you access to your data so that you can see what they've collected
on you and to check for errors. Not only is your information being
shared, but perhaps your incorrect information is being shared. And
hardly any companies tell you how you can have personal data
deleted from their systems.

States can enact their own privacy laws, and they can be more restrictive than the federal one—which frankly doesn't have the teeth it should. The right of states to do so was explicitly expressed in the financial modernization act. But few states have even contemplated the matter. California enacted a much tougher version in 2004, but portions of it got invalidated by subsequent court rulings. Still, the California measure does require opt-in consent before data can be sold to outside parties.

Opt-in rules remove the burden from the consumer, and that's why I'm all for them. If we had them nationwide, I feel certain that far less personal information would be floating around and getting scooped up by thieves.

Privacy Matters More Than a Free Toaster

So read your privacy statements and then evaluate the contents to decide who you want to do business with. Most people select their banks based on which one offers the highest interest rate on their savings account or what inviting incentive they dangle for you to open an account. But they ought to make these decisions based on who does a better job of protecting the information they entrust them with.

It's not enough that businesses establish privacy policies. They need to adhere to them. In 2003 Victoria's Secret settled a suit brought by the New York attorney general after it was found that personal information of customers was inadvertently made available on the lingerie company's website. This clearly violated the company's privacy policy, which specified that such information was kept on a secure server. Victoria's Secret had to vow to establish better security and provide 560 customers with appropriate compensation for the blunder.

If your bank doesn't offer the controls that it ought to, use another one. If a shopping site falls short in its privacy policy, shop at another place. Or complain vigorously about the policy, and maybe a miracle will happen and they'll rectify the deficiencies. That's what I do.

9

My Farewell to Checks

This is a chapter that I never expected to write. If you're going to be effective in battling crime, especially an opponent as durable as identity theft, you have to be both nimble and adaptable. That means revamping your strategies when conditions change. And so I want to explain the most significant about-face that I've made in trying to thwart identity thieves: saying farewell to checks.

Over the years I've made most of my money designing technologies that go into securing paper such as checks, car titles, and birth certificates. I designed the Supercheck, a high-security personal check manufactured with seventeen safety features. I also designed the SuperBusiness Check and SafeChecks for companies and municipalities that want extremely secure checks. Almost my entire life, in other words, has been connected to checks in an almost passionate way. I've always believed in checks, when they contain features that make them safer. And I've felt good about those safeguards I've established.

Whether we like it or not, the check is still a big part of our society and will be for some time to come. Checking accounts have existed in America since 1865. Experts believe that the check was actually invented by the Romans in 352 B.C. These days Americans write something like 39 billion checks a year. That figure is starting to come down a little bit, but the prevalence of checks is still huge.

The truth is, however, that I rarely write checks anymore, and I don't feel you should either. It's just too dangerous. Every check you write to the hairstylist or the cleaner has your name and signature, your bank's name and address, your account number, and your routing number. Salespeople routinely ask for a driver's license or work number, as well as other personal information, and scribble that on the check. These days you never get that check back. Was it shredded, or not? Did someone make a copy of it? Certainly just the check front alone contained more than enough information for someone to draft on your bank account—or become you.

I'd like to keep that information to myself. I've thought long and hard about this point, and my conclusion is, Why would you write a check today?

I prefer to walk into the supermarket and put my purchases on my credit card. Why should I use my money every month when I can leave it in the bank earning interest? I'll use the credit card's money. I pay the balance in full every month, and thus as long as I pay it within the "grace period," the card company doesn't charge me any interest. And I leave it with all the risk, since I have a full thirty days to question any suspect charge on my bill. Suppose I purchase a clock with a check and it doesn't work and the company says to me, "We're not refunding your money. We think it works." To get my money back, I have to sue the company in small claims court. But if I buy it on a credit card, I just tell the credit card company that I'm not paying for this, it doesn't work—I dispute it. And I have zero liability. If someone stands over my shoulder and steals my credit card number and uses it, I don't have to worry about what it's going to cost me.

Since I travel a great deal and have rather high expenses, I especially like those credit cards that give you money back after you spend a certain amount. Anytime someone wants to give me money for doing what I already do, I'll take it.

You can't entirely get away from checks, not yet at least. So I do write a check to pay my credit card bill and to pay my mortgage (which I would pay by credit card if they would accept it), because I know who's getting that check. But I would be much wiser to use a credit card. And not a debit card. A debit card is the same thing as money. You might as well write a check.

$99 Puts a Million Dollars at Risk

Ten years or so ago, if you had a brokerage account, Merrill Lynch or one of the other brokerage houses would give you a book of checks, but they would tell you that you couldn't write one for under $1,000. And you'd be limited to three or four checks a month or else there would be a charge, because they didn't want to be bothered with processing all those checks. And so people didn't regard those accounts as their primary checking account. They had another one at Chase or Citibank, and they used a Merrill check only if they had to write a big check out of their mutual fund account to buy a bedroom set or a car.

Then the brokerage houses changed their minds. They decided that they wanted to be like banks and have their customers write checks. Now they say, you can write as many checks as you like for any amount—we want this to be your primary checking account. You can write a $10 check to the pizza parlor or a $30 check to the babysitter. And in fact, whereas the bank charges you $18 for a box of checks, the brokerage house will provide you with all the checks you want for free. Therefore you're inclined to use the brokerage's checks.

Think again. You go to the luggage store and write a check for $99 on your checking account, which contains $1,400 or $2,200. If someone tries to rip you off, that's the most that can be stolen. But with a brokerage check you are writing a $99 check, or even a $25 check, on a brokerage account that contains half a million dollars or a quarter of a million—your whole life's savings. Would you like identity thieves to have access to that? Your exposure is vastly greater, and it ought to give you pause. It sure gives me pause, so I would use the credit card that the brokerage house issued to you rather than its checks.

Sweeter Than Halloween

October 28, 2004, was an important date for identity thieves, one of those seminal moments that they probably circled on their calendar, licking their chops in anticipation. No, it wasn't simply three days before Halloween, a reminder to get a costume. This was Check 21 Day, and for crooks it was a lot sweeter than any Halloween candy.

Like most consumers, you probably didn't pay much attention to the passage of the Check Clearing for the 21st Century Act, known informally as Check 21. Unless you were in the banking business or a check aficionado like myself, it was just one more federal law in the avalanche of legislation that erupts out of Congress. The law had perfectly good intentions and was designed to benefit

financial institutions and consumers alike. Unfortunately, it also af-
forded a delectable benefit for crooks, and they didn't even have to
lobby for it.

Check 21 is aimed at hastening the processing of checks in the
United States. That's a noble enough goal—who hasn't been frustrated and aggravated by waiting three to ten business days until a
check clears and the funds are made available for use?

The tired old way in which checks cleared involved banks physically sending the actual paper checks to one another. A check deposited in one bank was put on an airplane and then a truck took it
to the paying bank. This typically required a day or two, and it might
be a few days longer before the bank authorized the release of funds.
That was slow going in today's fast-moving world, when people get
annoyed if it takes more than fifteen seconds to connect to the Internet. And it was costly for the banks involved.

Check 21's answer is an entirely new financial creation called
the *image reproduction document*, or more simply the *substitute
check*. It's a paper reproduction of a real check that, if it satisfies the
requirements of Check 21, becomes a legal equivalent of the original check. Those requirements are that it contains an image of
the front and back of the check; contains an MICR line (the string
of digits and symbols at the bottom of checks) with the same information as the MICR line of the check; conforms in paper stock and
dimensions with industry standards; and can be processed automatically.

All checks with the exception of foreign checks are eligible to
become substitute checks: consumer checks, business checks, government checks, traveler's checks, money orders, and drafts.

Check 21 doesn't insist that checks be exchanged electronically, but it does encourage it. Thus it facilitates check *truncation*, the removal of the paper check from the check-processing system. In short, banks no longer have to send the actual checks that have been deposited to the paying bank; nor do they have to send them back to the account holders after they've been cashed. That means that checks can clear on the same day that they are deposited, though that doesn't mean banks have to shorten their hold times on funds. In other words, banks may save money, but they don't have to pass the savings along to you.

While a substitute check is the legal equivalent of an original check, it is less than helpful when fraud enters the picture. Since it can't be used to determine things like pen pressure or to analyze handwriting effectively, it is much less useful in proving forgery or alteration. The actual instrument of the fraud, the original paper check, is typically destroyed—and there goes the evidence.

Another worry is that when the original check is transformed back and forth between paper and electronic formats, opportunities exist for the amount on the paper check to be changed when it's turned into an electronic image for processing. What if these images are accessed by thieves? Large-scale fraud is a legitimate worry.

Banks post these electronic images on customers' online accounts as a service to them. But that too poses significant risks. If someone penetrates your online banking account, not only do they have the ability to replicate your check perfectly, but they also have your account number and your signature. If the store accepting your check took your driver's license number and date of birth and scribbled it on the front or back of the check, they have that as well.

Banks don't get the fact that an online archive of check images beats an actual checkbook any day. Placing both check images and monthly statements online offers identity thieves information on both the visual aspects of the checks and the behavioral history of the account. These days banks have detection systems programmed to notice variations in how checks look and to pick up on unusual check-writing behavior. If someone starts writing far more checks than usual, or in higher amounts, these systems flag the account.

But by accessing your online account, a criminal now has context. The thief can study your spending history, going back weeks and months, and then roughly adhere to that pattern to evade detection. He can make a reliable estimate of what check number you will likely use next, another guard against getting caught.

Gangs in Eastern Europe have launched phishing scams that trick consumers into relinquishing their log-in and password information for their online accounts. Then, armed with monthly statements and check images, they produce counterfeit checks identical in appearance and written for an amount appropriate for the account, bearing a scanned signature.

Another problem with image-based detection systems stems from the limitations of current check readers. Check 21 requires that the converting financial institution provide warranties that the substitute check includes all the information contained on the original check. Existing check readers can scan only at resolutions approaching 240 dpi, while even consumer-grade printers and copiers operate at 600 dpi or above. Existing check readers are thus inherently unable to distinguish between the appearance of an original item and a copy produced on such equipment.

It would help a lot if banks blocked the MICR line and the signature line on check images that are sent online to customers. For that matter, why not block the name as well?

Banks could easily accomplish this if they were willing to spend a little money. Ori Eisen, a friend of mine, is the head of 41st Parameter, a company that sells Internet fraud solutions to banks and merchants. (The company name is based on the idea that if the same forty parameters—like name, address, etc.—are used to detect and prevent fraud, then whoever uses the forty-first has a distinct edge.) He has developed software that will mask portions of the check that reveal personal information, including the name and signature and areas where identification information might be recorded. You'll still see 75 percent of the check, enough to recognize it as yours. Could a thief unblur the masked sections? Ori's answer: "You can't unscramble scrambled eggs."

For the most part, however, banks don't want to make even this small effort to protect their customers. When you tell them about this threat, they get defensive and say, hey, in the old world criminals swiped checkbooks from people, and in the modern online world checks are protected by passwords. Cracking passwords hasn't deterred sophisticated thieves, and they much prefer getting at an account online to pilfering a checkbook out of a woman's handbag while she shops at Macy's.

At Least the Security Features Still Work

As long as we have checks, Check 21 doesn't diminish the value of security features. While the search for image-survivable features continues, the only solution that protects both the banks and their customers is one that makes it possible to recognize a fake when it's presented. Thus consumers should use high-security checks with eight or more security features.

If you're going to write a check to pay the electric bill or the gas bill, don't put it in your mailbox outside your house. Typically people put their outgoing mail in the mailbox and put the flag up, which is sort of like raising a red flag. It makes you vulnerable to an extremely common scam called *washing checks*. There are criminals who drive through neighborhoods early in the morning, see that red flag, and remove the envelope containing your check to the electric company.

They take that check home, put a piece of Scotch tape over your signature, front and back, and drop it into a cake pan. They pour over it an everyday household chemical that we all have in our homes that removes all ink from paper except printer's ink (for example, base ink). Thus anything you typed, printed from a computer, or signed with a ballpoint or felt-tip pen dissolves quickly. The criminals can thereby wash off all the information on that check except for your signature. The $109 check you wrote to the electric company comes out to be a blank check signed by you, because the Scotch tape protects the signature from the chemical. They can make the check out to themselves, fill in any amount, and cash it.

So if you're going to mail a check, take it directly to the post office mailbox and mail it there. An even better precaution is to use a pen with permanent ink. I use a Uni-ball 207 gel pen, black, because its pigment ink actually goes into the paper. It costs me under $2. When I write checks with it, I never have to worry about anyone using chemicals to wash the information off. No chemicals on earth can remove gels from paper. That's a simple method you can use to protect yourself from having your checks washed.

To a large extent, checks are a generational thing. People in their fifties or sixties have the custom well ingrained in them and tend to write a lot of checks, while younger people don't, other than to pay their rent or credit card bills. So I'm preaching to those who do habitually write a lot of checks to wise up, drastically cut back, and go with plastic rather than paper. And since everyone has to write a few checks each month, make sure they're extremely secure ones.

10

They Got Me—Now What?

Your turn may come. No matter how many precautions you take, you too might become the victim of identity theft. And when it happens, you usually don't know what to do. And why would you? You're traumatized, confused, and mad. You may also feel ashamed. The experience is not unlike when someone breaks into your house. Even if nothing valuable has been stolen, some stranger has trespassed without your permission, and you feel outraged and violated. Well, in this case, someone has invaded your identity. The feeling can be even more wrenching.

It's important, though, to calm down and collect yourself, then follow an orderly protocol. Here are the steps to take.

1. Call the credit bureau fraud departments. Report the crime to the three credit bureaus so that they can put an alert on your file. As I mentioned earlier, it will serve as a signal to businesses to be wary next time "you" apply for credit. The alert means that any creditor, prior to granting new credit, has to call you at a number of your choosing. I'd pick a cell phone or pager where you can always be reached.

You should also have them place a victim statement on your reports. This is a word of explanation from you, and it should say something like: "My identifying information has been used to commit fraud. Please call me at [give your phone number] to verify all applications."

These measures will make it more difficult for you to obtain credit as well—but that's the point. If it's a hassle for you, it should be close to impossible for a thief.

To make matters less complicated for once, one phone call will do the job of notifying all three credit bureaus. The law requires them to inform one another, and fraud alerts will be put on all three reports. Initial alerts stay on for ninety days, or you can get an extended alert, which lasts for seven years. Be sure to take that into consideration. If your situation was minor and easily cleared up, you may not want a fraud alert on your record for that lengthy a period of time, since it does make it harder for you to get credit.

Here is the contact information for the credit bureau fraud departments:

Equifax
www.equifax.com
800-525-6285
P.O. Box 105069
Atlanta, GA 30398

Experian
www.experian.com

888-397-3742

P.O. Box 9532

Allen, TX 75013

TransUnion

www.transunion.com

800-680-7289

Fraud Victim Assistance Department

P.O. Box 6790

Fullerton, CA 92834

When you notify the bureaus, you'll receive a complimentary copy of each credit report, and you're allowed two free reports within a year if you request an extended fraud alert. When they arrive, check them scrupulously to make sure you're aware of all the fraud that has occurred. Correct all mistakes, following the procedure I spelled out in Chapter 7.

2. Shut down all compromised accounts and documents. In this step you fix your credit and get it back to normal. Immediately pull the plug on the old and the new, both your own accounts that the thief may have been misusing and any new accounts that he opened in your name. Include credit card companies and service providers like your phone company, Internet provider, and utilities. One thief restricted his stealing to opening up electronic accounts for phone service and cable TV. When you reopen your accounts, make sure you have a new account number, and guard it with a fresh password. You can protect your reputation by asking the creditor to classify the old account as "closed at the customer's request." The other option—"card lost or stolen"—can make you look careless, even though it wasn't your fault.

Your maximum liability under federal law for unauthorized use of your credit card is $50 per card. If you report the loss before your card is actually used by a criminal, then you aren't responsible for any unauthorized charges. Plus, you aren't liable if your credit card number, but not the card, was stolen. Some banks and card companies offer zero liability, even if the thief has already hit the mall with your card.

Closing accounts that were yours to begin with is pretty easy. The hard part is erasing the charges that you didn't make, and closing accounts that the thief opened. Ask to speak to the fraud department of the bank, retailer, or credit card company, and find out what forms you need to dispute fraudulent charges and accounts. You may be able to use the ID Theft Affidavit, a standard form available from the FTC (you can download it off their website) that serves as a three-page master key to identity theft repair. Many companies accept the affidavit as a fraud dispute form. Some, though, continue to require the company's own forms. For now, go on record about everything you are disputing, and have the forms you need sent to you. Be sure to follow up these calls in writing to make things extra-official. If you're dealing with a new account, get as much documentation about it as you can, such as a copy of the application used to open the account and transaction records. If the creditor is uncooperative, it's probably because of its security policy. Imagine the irony of that! Keep trying, and see if the police will help.

From the time you receive the credit card statement listing a fraudulent charge, you have sixty days to dispute that charge. This is true even if the thief changed your address and you never actually received the statement listing the $5,000 he spent on the walnut bookcases. When you write to the credit card company, include your name, account number, and a detailed list of the fraudulent charges, including the date and the amount. Make sure you address the letter to the billing inquiry department, and send it certified mail, return receipt requested. Don't forget to include all relevant documentation.

The credit card company has thirty days to let you know that it received your letter, and it must resolve the dispute within two billing cycles, a maximum of ninety days.

Once it does correct the matter, get a letter from the card company that says that the charges were fraudulent and that they have been removed. Hang on to the original of this letter, and include a copy whenever you write to a credit bureau or debt collector. You'll want to get the same type of letter when you shut down bad credit accounts that the thief opened in your name.

If your ATM or debit card has been lost or stolen, again report the theft to your bank as soon as possible, cancel the card, and get a new card with a different PIN. Your liability here depends on how fast you report the loss. If you report it within two business days after you've realized that the card is missing, you won't be held responsible for more than $50. If you report it after more than two days but fewer than sixty, you could lose up to $500. If you fail to report an unauthorized transfer within sixty days of receiving the bank statement that contains the loss, you could be liable for unlimited losses. Some debit card companies, however, voluntarily cap your liability at $50, same as a credit card.

Your financial institution has ten days to investigate your case, three days to notify you of the result, and one day to fix the error once they've finished the investigation. If it takes longer than that, they must return the money to your account while they investigate, for up to forty-five days. They'll want that money back if they find out you really did spend it, but they have to notify you in writing first.

So generally you're not out a lot of money, unless through phishing techniques or other means a thief actually gets access to your bank accounts and takes your money. Trying to get the bank to give you the physical money to put back into your bank account is a much bigger process. And then we get into laws and liability issues. Questions will have to be answered such as: What did you do to make it difficult for someone to steal from you? Did you use due diligence, or were you reckless?

Under Regulation E, the federal rule that governs electronic transfers, banks have to refund money that has been fraudulently transferred from their accounts, if you tell the bank within sixty days of receiving your bank statement. Some banks will go further and guarantee *zero liability*, similar to credit card protection.

If the identity thief stole checks, call the bank and stop payment on any outstanding checks that you didn't write. Close out those accounts directly with the bank. Open new accounts that are protected by passwords. Then contact the check verification services so they can tell their retailers not to accept checks from the thief. In the future, have check orders delivered to your local branch and pick them up there, rather than have them mailed to your home.

If you find a fraudulent charge on a legitimate account, federal law states that you have sixty days from the date a creditor sends a bill statement to you to inform the creditor of the fraudulent charge. Accounts are sometimes hijacked so the billing address is changed. This allows the thief to conceal his tracks. In these cases you need to advise the creditor that you never got a bill. It's always best to call the creditor directly first, then follow up that conversation in writing.

If you haven't been getting bills from a company, go to the local post office and inquire whether a change of address has been put in place. If it has, file a complaint with the postmaster, who might be at the local office or at another location. If no change of address has been enacted but you think your mail might have been stolen, then contact the Postal Inspector's Office. He may want you to file a police report before recording the case.

If your driver's license has been stolen or you believe it is being used fraudulently, contact your local Department of Motor Vehicles. The process to get this rectified varies by state.

If your passport has been lost or stolen, you must contact the State Department (www.state.gov), which has a lost or stolen section in its passport services. To replace the passport, you have to go in person to a passport agency or acceptance facility.

Fraud committed in investment accounts comes under the bailiwick of the Securities and Exchange Commission (SEC). If you believe your account has been tampered with, notify the investment company's fraud department, so the account is frozen, and then a new account and password will be established. Follow up the phone conversation with a written notice. Then report the matter to the SEC, which has an online complaint center (www.sec.gov/complaint.shtml).

If someone has declared bankruptcy in your name, write to the U.S. Trustee in the region where the filing was made. A list of the U.S. Trustee Program's regions can be found at www.usdoj.gov/ust, or in the Blue Pages of your phone book under U.S. Government—Bankruptcy Administration.

In cases where you suspect someone got a job under your identity and therefore is reporting fraudulent income, contact the Social Security Administration, and get a copy of your Social Security Statement of Contributions. It lists all income earned under your Social Security number. If a thief managed to get a job using your number, then when you file your tax return, the IRS will think that you are not reporting all your income and are underpaying your taxes.

If you do find there has been a fraud, ask the Social Security Administration for a Detailed Earnings Statement. Review it to identify the employer, then contact him about the fraud and request that he correct the false income. You also should call the IRS and tell them to have the income removed from your Social Security number. The changes made with the Social Security Administration may be sufficient for them to delete the income, or the IRS may ask you to send them a letter explaining how you couldn't have earned the false income, such as the extremely difficult commute in holding two full-time jobs simultaneously, one in Maine and one in Nebraska.

3. File a police report. The point of filing a police report is not necessarily to catch the thief. Most thieves are not going to be caught or even pursued. But the report will help you remove the fraud from your credit report. Throughout the process of recovering your identity, you're likely to be met with skepticism. Companies will want some kind of proof that you really are a victim rather than a deadbeat trying to get out of paying your debts. A police report is the best proof you can offer, because creditors assume you wouldn't file a police report unless you really meant it.

A police report will also protect you if someone tries to get a passport in your name. Passport agencies check all applicants against a national database to see if any criminal activities or duplicate passports are associated with them. A police report of a stolen identity will flag your name in that database.

If you don't know where your identity was stolen—which is the case in most thefts—then file the report with your local police department. If you do know where it happened—visiting your daughter at college in Chicago or while vacationing in Orlando—then file the report with that local police department.

The problem is, it's often extremely difficult, if not impossible, to get the police to take you seriously. Many local police departments aren't going to be interested, especially if all you had stolen were documents to which you can't assign a value. Be persistent. Explain that without a police report, you have no way to stop the theft from continuing or repair your credit. Give the police copies of any documentation you already have, like your credit report, debt collection letters, or the ID Theft Affidavit.

If the local police still refuse to help you, which does happen all too frequently, try the county police, and if you're still getting nowhere, go to the state police.

When you file the report, be certain that it lists every instance of fraud that was committed using your identifying information. And make sure you get a copy of it, so you can send copies to creditors. When you do that, it's helpful to include the phone number of the investigating officer. If you absolutely cannot get a copy of the police report, at least obtain the report number and ask for a letter stating that the report couldn't be given to you.

4. Establish good records—of everything! Send all letters certified mail, return receipt requested, from your local post office.

That way you'll have a record of when you sent something and when it was received. To play it extra safe, ask the people you speak to for written confirmation of your conversations. If they refuse, you can write to them (certified mail, return receipt requested) and list what was said. Ask them to write back if anything is incorrect. If they don't reply, that can serve as your confirmation.

Keep a copy of every letter and form you send, as well as the original of every piece of paper you didn't generate, like police reports, credit reports, and letters you receive. Also maintain a log of everything you do—every letter you send and receive, every phone call you make. With phone calls, jot down the names of the people you spoke to, their title, and their phone number; what you discussed; what they agreed to do and when; what they need from you and when. If the person you speak to doesn't help you, record that, and ask to speak to someone else.

Follow up all phone calls and face-to-face conversations in writing. The people you talk to at credit card companies and law enforcement agencies may deal with hundreds of calls just like yours every day. Even if they sound reassuring on the phone, they might forget you the moment they hang up, and it's only your word against theirs that you ever spoke. Putting things in writing will jog some memories and give you proof that the communication actually occurred.

You may want to keep track of your costs, in case your thief is caught. Your chances of getting some money back are much better if you maintain a log and save your receipts. Eligible expenditures may include: phone calls, postage, mileage, legal assistance, notarizing, court costs for documentation, time lost from work, organizational and reference materials, and personal assistance like a babysitter or an accountant.

Use a filing system that will give you ready access to everything you need. Hang on to these files, even after you think the ordeal is over, because identity theft can strike anew at any time.

5. File a complaint with the FTC. Finally, once you've determined as best you can the extent of the fraud, file a complaint with the Federal Trade Commission, which can be done online at www.consumer.gov/idtheft, or by phone at 1-877-IDTHEFT. The FTC doesn't get involved in resolving individual cases, but the complaint is useful information in its work to investigate fraud, and it could spur a law enforcement response.

I also recommend that you report the case to the FBI. In most instances, they aren't going to do anything. In general, the FBI is concerned with national, large-scale fraud, crime patterns, and organized-crime activity. Nonetheless, your report, added to those of others that come in, may assist them in those more comprehensive efforts. At www.fbi.gov you can find the number of the FBI field office for your area. Call and let them know what transpired. You can also report your case online at www.tips.fbi.gov.

If Your Thief Is Wanted

If an identity thief has been arrested for a crime using your name, or if there's a warrant out for him, you need to follow a whole additional series of steps. These instances are a lot trickier than others, and the results are rarely entirely satisfactory.

There is no standard national protocol to extricate yourself from a criminal justice database. How cumbersome the process is depends on the state. Start by filling out an impersonation report with the police department or court that made the arrest or issued the warrant. While you're there, have your identity undeniably established by getting the police to take your fingerprints and photograph. Make a point of having them copy your driver's license and passport. Your impersonator may have a phony driver's license and passport in your name, but he won't look like you or have your fingerprints. If the crook was caught in another town or state—or country—ask the local police to forward the impersonation report to the law enforcement agency in that jurisdiction. Following up is imperative—lots of things get lost in the bureaucratic shuffle.

If things go the way they should (unfortunately, they don't always go that way), the agency will eventually cancel any warrants and, if you were arrested or booked, will issue a clearance letter that absolves you. Don't simply file it away. From then on, I'm afraid, you will have to carry this document with you to avoid humiliating experiences. If you find yourself wrongly arrested or even stopped for a common traffic infraction, this is the sole proof you'll have to show the cops that you're not a hunted drug dealer or wanted for armed robbery. And pray that they'll recognize it and assume that it's authentic.

I know this doesn't sound like much of a solution, that you should go to all that trouble and yet a policeman could still associate you with crimes committed by your identity clone and haul you down to the station. It's an awful part of the lingering residue of this form of identity theft.

Unfortunately your name, once it has been inserted in a criminal database, is probably not going to be completely stricken from the official record. Law enforcement doesn't erase names easily. One useful thing you can do to lower your profile a bit is to demand that the *key name* be switched from yours to the thief's real name. In many cases, of course, the police don't know the crook's actual identity, and he may have multiple guises, so in those instances insist that it be changed to a variation like John Doe or Jane Doe. It's better than your name. Once they've done that, your name should be mentioned as an alias and nothing more. Not the perfect solution, but it helps.

Clear your name in court records as well. Check with your state to find out its steps for so doing, or call the DA's office in the county where the case was handled. It should be able to furnish you with the court records that you will have to submit to correct the matter. It's a complicated process, much more difficult than straightening out your credit, and you may find it best to retain a criminal defense attorney to assist you. In this area it's worth the expense to do all that you can to restore your good name and keep the law off your back.

The sad truth is that under current laws your chance of entirely getting that crime off your record is almost none.

Let the Pros Help You

All of this sounds like a lot of work, and it is, especially since you haven't done anything wrong. The reality is, you can talk to all the friends in the world, you can even talk to your bank and your credit card company, but those employees are not paid to help you, and they're not going to take the interest that someone who is being paid to help you will. So unless yours is a simple case, I strongly recommend that you hire a resolution service. They deal with thousands of cases a day, of all stripes, and help thousands of people to recover their credit. Let me be clear—they can't do everything. When it comes to bankruptcy and criminal records, they can give you some guidance, but most of the burden in those sticky areas is going to be yours.

The whole resolution arena is a fast-growing industry, and you can be sure it has its cast of shady operators and profiteers too. Keep your eyes open, and don't trust anyone who lacks a reliable track record that you can check. If you enroll in the PrivacyGuard program, you are automatically furnished a resolution service, one that knows what it's doing.

Repelling the Debt Collectors

Even after you've done all the legwork, it can take time before your records are completely straightened out. Bill collectors may still hound you. Exercise your rights. The law states that if you write and ask a debt collector to leave you alone, they have to do just that. Afterward all they can do is contact you to tell you that they aren't going to call you anymore—fat chance of that—or that they're going to undertake some action against you.

If that action is something distinctly unpleasant, your best course of action is to write to the collection agency, within thirty days of receiving the notice, and inform them that you don't actually owe the debt and are the victim. Explain about the identity theft, and supply them with your documentation.

If they still hector you, they must provide you with proof that you owe the debt. What tends to happen is that the debt will be referred back to the original creditor. Simply follow the procedures mentioned above to clear it up.

Debts these days get sold from collection agency to collection agency, and many victims find that just when they think they've satisfied the problem, a new and more obnoxious collector sprouts up and starts harassing them. Whoever buys debt is supposed to check into the history, but frequently they're so anxious to annoy the debtor that they don't bother. So quickly set them straight, the way you did the original collector. Be blunt, the way they are, and get them off your back.

11

The Crime That Keeps on Stealing

Sandra Stiverson, of Conroe, Texas, wrote a check for her phone bill and dropped it in the mailbox. Nothing unusual about that—she did it every month. But the check bounced, and that was a first for Sandra. Next thing she knew, her husband was online poring over their checking account. As he sifted through the canceled checks, he looked up and asked her about a check for $900 made out to a name he didn't recognize (I'll call her Barbara Z. Tonroy). It puzzled him. It puzzled her.

"I never bounced a check before in my life, and I've never written one for nine hundred dollars," Sandra told me. "And I'd never heard of anyone with that name."

She was going to hear that name a lot. Even though she "got on the ball and went down to the police station" to take care of the mess, more and more checks would come back—twenty-seven of them, amounting to $6,516.21. Maybe it was not a huge amount in the ugly universe of identity theft, but in her universe it was a staggering amount.

Sandra endured all the hassles and frustrations that accompany identity theft. She took all the right steps to correct the situation. But the constant brush-off she got from the police really got her Texas temper going. "I had to become my own investigator," she said. "I'm very bummed out, because they've done nothing on this. The FBI doesn't care, the four or five police stations I've dealt with don't do anything!"

No one was arrested, and no suspects were even questioned, despite the fact that Sandra on her own tracked down an actual person named Barbara Z. Tonroy, who was living in Dallas, and several stores caught the person using that name on surveillance cameras. A number of employees at the establishments where the fake checks were cashed have told her they can identify the crook. Sandra said witnesses have described her car, a spiffy Cadillac (wonder who paid for that!), but unfortunately no one got the license plate number.

"Understand that the woman using my name is an overweight black woman, well over six feet tall with glasses, and I am five foot four, skinny as a rail, with long blond hair," Sandra said.

Sandra felt a bit like the famous western sheriff in a complacent tumbleweed town going it alone to get justice done. Digging into county records, she located a photo of a Dallas house in the name of Barbara Z. Tonroy. She has considered going to confront the woman, but is a little afraid to try that on her own; plus, Dallas is a four-hour drive away.

The Dallas police could have helped, but that apparently was asking too much. "The Dallas police told me that there is really nothing they can do until a merchant files a police report, because I am not considered the 'victim,' the merchant is," she said. "However, I did not give up and continued to call them until they finally told me they would call the person whose name appears on forged checks to see if she will agree to take a polygraph test. After three months of 'phone tag,' supposedly she has agreed to. Why are they resorting only to a polygraph test when various stores have her on surveillance, two Kroger stores have her thumbprint, and Discount Tire has two employees who could possibly ID her?"

At last report Barbara had not taken the lie detector test to which she consented. As a private eye, Sandra was making some inroads, but they all seemed to lead to a place called frustration. During one close call she talked to a J.C. Penney store employee who said he recalled the thief and that he would file a police report. "I said I could kiss your feet," she told me. "But then when I called him back, he said because we don't have her on film, and she was just browsing the store, the police said it's not worth it."

More than three years have lapsed. The ongoing ordeal has frustrated Sandra and left her edgy; it has exposed her to public humiliations that she doesn't deserve. "It's caused me and my family a lot of grief and stress and some money in trying to clear my name with several merchants and creditors," she said. "I tried to buy school clothes at Sears for my daughter recently, and they wouldn't take my check. They said Telecheck, who collects for Sears, said, 'You write bad checks.'"

She is alternately mad and sad and just plain confused. One day identity theft came visiting, and it refused to leave.

The Fear That Won't End

The dark side of identity theft is that it doesn't necessarily end, even when you take the steps I recommended in the last chapter. You're dealing with persistent criminals who don't relent and an imperfect resolution system. That combination makes it very hard to completely come out from under this insidious crime.

The consequence of identity theft is much more than the loss of dollars and of time spent on restoring your credit. Identity theft is like a chronic disease. It often occurs in more than one episode, and it keeps on hurting. Rarely is justice done, even when you go and track down the thief yourself, and so the crime instills fear that doesn't quickly abate. Even after one particular thief appears to be finished stealing your money, he continues to steal your sense of security. Since there's little chance he's going to be apprehended, you're always nervous that he'll return—and he might. Suppose your thief does get caught. You don't know if he acted alone or in concert with co-conspirators. Did he sell your identity to others? Did they then use it and sell it to others? Given these cycles, once you've been violated, it's hard to feel safe again.

That queasy feeling can persist for a very long time—in fact, a lifetime. The emotional impact can be more serious than the financial impact, which often is negligible or nonexistent. Some victims like Stone Tyler, whom we met in Chapter 1, actually change their names or Social Security numbers to find peace of mind, but that can be an ordeal. Some couples have been pushed to the brink of divorce by the stress. Or over the brink. I've heard about a number of divorces whose central cause was the residue of identity theft. What price do you put on the psychological torment of this crime? On being left insecure? On being unable to sleep well? On losing a marriage?

The lingering aftertaste of identity theft that people like Sandra feel is one of the major reasons I care so much about stopping this epidemic. This crime keeps on stealing—from your psyche and sense of well-being. I think it's worth hearing about a few experiences, so you can appreciate how important it is to never have this happen to you in the first place.

"No, I'm Not a Pimp"

In 2003 Paul Fairchild had just moved to California and begun a job doing website work for the Boy Scouts of America. Teetering under the financial burden of having relocated his family from New York, he was watching expenses pretty carefully.

The family was invited to a wedding in Oregon. But when he went to rent a tux, he was surprised that his American Express credit card was turned down. In addition, he was later informed, the bills were past due on the corporate cards held by his business, the Ebony Passion Escort Service.

Come again? he thought. An escort service? He had never heard of it. He was a straitlaced website designer, not a pimp.

He made it clear to American Express that a thief had been living a swinging lifestyle at his expense, but he nevertheless began getting bills for such pricey purchases as Manolo Blahnik spike heels, which he never would have looked good in. "The cost of those shoes would have paid my rent for two months in the California apartment my family and I had just relocated to," he said. His wife, Rachel, had been agonizing over whether spending $15 for their son's Payless shoes for the wedding was going to throw the family budget into shock.

Fairchild, who is in his mid-thirties, estimates that a thief ran up $1 million worth of bills in his name, including a mortgage on an apartment building in Brooklyn. He doesn't know who did it, but he suspects the tenant who moved into his old New York apartment. "I think he got some mail delivered there in my name," he said. "A couple of months after the guy moves in, he drops off the radar screen completely, then the fraudulent stuff starts. There's a whole lot of circumstantial stuff. I wish I could afford to hire the detectives to prove this, but I can't."

Fairchild wasn't held liable for the unauthorized spending spree, but his cost was considerable in the anguish and time— sometimes a full forty hours a week—spent trying to straighten out the mess, as well as about $3,000 in lawyers' fees. Just to make his life more miserable, the bank that held the false building mortgage even sued him at one point.

He was profoundly unhappy about the response from American Express. "You know that ad they have on TV, about where you're in South America and your luggage is lost and you're supposed to call American Express and they move mountains to take care of you?" he said. "Well the truth is, they don't do much."

The minute his tuxedo rental was turned down and he found out about the dubious escort service bills in his name, he called American Express. "It was a weekend, so they said call back Monday," he said. "I thought that sounded a little like closing the barn door after the cow has gotten out. I said okay but put a fraud alert on this right now. They said get the papers notarized, certified, etc. So pretty soon I started getting calls from a rude debt collector. After about the fifth call I said it's not my problem, and he said he kept seeing more charges from between when I asked for the fraud alert and the time when American Express was finally doing something. It was about twenty-five hundred dollars more. That's how serious American Express is about this. Sure, they're losing money, but did you ever wonder why the credit card companies charge twenty-four-point-nine percent interest or whatever on the credit?"

Three years after the crime, the disruption continues. "It's tapered off, but I still get bills for things, especially fake cell phone accounts," Fairchild said. "It's gotten so crazy with one cell phone company. They keep telling me I've opened up new accounts, when I haven't."

Reburying the Dead

Imagine the agony involved if you're forced to clear the name of someone you've lost, either recently or at some time deep in the past. It's not that your deceased relative needs his credit rating restored; he's someplace where credit doesn't matter. But revisiting your grief can be excruciatingly painful and traumatic.

In May 2002 a woman got a notice from the police in North Carolina, saying that her husband had been cited for a traffic violation. She was at once shocked and infused with renewed hope. She had thought her husband died in the World Trade Center on September 11. But his remains hadn't been confirmed—was it possible he had somehow survived? Unfortunately it wasn't. When she contacted the police, she learned that an illegal immigrant had created a false driver's license so that he could live and work as her deceased husband.

She was convulsed with sorrow all over again—and extremely angry at this desecration of her husband's memory.

An elderly couple had a registered nurse living with them for years, caring for the man, who was sickly. When he died, the nurse left—along with his identity. When his widow wrote a check for his funeral, it bounced, because the nurse had already cleaned out his account.

It's worst when we're talking about a child. A Virginia mother tragically lost her six-year-old daughter in a car accident in 1982. No parent ever completely recuperates from the death of a child, especially when it happens at such a young age. Out of the blue, nineteen years later she learned that her daughter's identity had been assumed by a thief in order to enter the military reserves and who knows what else.

Understandably, she was terribly distraught, and who could possibly blame her? She felt as if someone had unburied her child and she now needed to bury her again. The past waves of shock and anguish returned full bore to torment her.

Criminal Records Live Forever

When thieves commit other crimes in your name, you really face a burden that won't go away. It's easy enough to check your credit record, but there's no easy way to check your criminal record. If an identity thief has put a blot on your record, you don't know it until the police stop you. And you never know when it's going to reappear. I'll tell you my own story.

A few years ago one of my sons had just graduated from college in Kansas. Before he started law school in Chicago, he was working as a park ranger, and so I told him I'd rent a U-Haul and move his stuff from Lawrence, Kansas, to his new apartment. I called a friend of mine in Arizona and asked him if he'd do the move with me on a weekend, and he readily agreed. We got an early start, and the first day we drove as far as Iowa. We stopped for dinner at six and were in bed by eight. Then the next morning we were tooling down the Interstate, and just as we entered Illinois, a state trooper pulled us over. I was doing fifty-five and had my seatbelt on. What could be the problem? The trooper came over and said, "I suppose you're wondering why I stopped you."

I said that I was.

"You know, you looked a little sleepy to me."

I told him not at all, we had gone to bed at eight and had just gotten up. He asked for my license and went to his car.

I wondered how he could have thought I was sleepy. He had been sitting in a ditch on the side of the road when I went by. In any event, he returned and asked me to come with him to his car. He said he wanted to play something and have me comment on it. He got on the radio and asked if there were any warrants or arrests for me. A girl responded by reading: arrest for forgery, arrest in France, the whole litany, along with the years, 1967, 1968, and so on.

I told him that everything was true, but I hoped that he noticed the dates. "I was a teenager," I said. "That was a long time ago."

"Well, what are you carrying in the truck?"

I told him.

He wanted to know if my friend would confirm what I had said, and I assured him he would. The trooper got out and asked my friend to confirm, and he did. Then the officer wanted to search the truck. I told him fine. Before he began, he asked if he'd find any firearms, drugs, or most important of all, counterfeiting tools. I said no.

About forty-five minutes had gone by already. It was about 95 degrees outside.

After he searched everything and found nothing, he asked me what I did for a living. I told him I was a consultant and worked for the FBI and taught at the FBI Academy. He asked what kind of fool I took him for.

I gave him the names and phone numbers of people he could call to confirm this, but that was apparently too much trouble. Then I showed him a brochure, because I was going to speak the next day at an FBI conference. The brochure identified me as the keynote speaker along with the commissioner of Scotland Yard. He looked a little worried and said, "I guess you are who you said you are."

He said I could go, then changed his mind and indicated that he was going to give me a warning ticket for speeding. I told him that I hadn't been speeding. Then he said, "You must know why I stopped you."

I didn't.

He said, "Profiling. We're looking for meth labs, and they usually are transported in U-Hauls by middle-aged men who are well dressed."

So the thing is, I engaged in some regrettable acts forty years ago, and they're still reaching out of the past to haunt me. When an identity thief attaches a criminal record to your name, it will always be sitting there, poised to catch you in its grip. Right now there is only one effective solution, and that's not to get a criminal record.

Like Opening a Pillow

For Trudy Aikens (not her real name), identity theft came visiting in the mid-1990s. Petite, dark-eyed Trudy arrived in New York from Kentucky to work in the fashion retailing business. She loved her job and loved working in the glamorous area near Grand Central Station, which was even more festive during the Christmas season. Of course, many companies hire temporary people to help out during this hectic time, and her company was one of them.

An employee in the accounting department mentioned that her sister would be glad to pick up a little extra holiday money by joining the firm through the end of the fiscal year. The harried executives were grateful not to have to go through a search process. Not only did they skip the interview but also the usual employee credit and background check.

In no time, she had selected her victim: Trudy. Trudy was one of three people in the company who had authority to sign checks, so her signature was on file. The new temporary employee began by signing Trudy's name to a check. Fortunately, an alert employee at Sterling National Bank caught it. "They called me and said the reason we suspected it was fraudulent was because I usually use my middle initial in signing checks," she said.

The bank suggested Trudy sift through the corporate checks. "There were six missing!" she said. "It didn't take an Einstein to figure out that it had to be someone from the company."

Because Trudy's employer was filing charges, the police came in and started doing security and background checks. "Banks have security cameras," Trudy said. "But they couldn't pin this situation on the employee, because she wasn't the one on camera."

So she must have been working with other people, it was decided.

Life went on, until Trudy received a credit card in the mail from Macy's: "I called and said what the heck, I didn't ask for a credit card. It turned out that someone had opened a credit account in my name. And she ran up a bill of five thousand dollars."

That was just the beginning. The thief proceeded to a mall in New Jersey and opened up five other credit card accounts.

Trudy called the detective who was investigating the corporate theft. He gave her the name and address of the suspected thief. It turned out she was part of an identity theft ring and was having other people—including the temporary worker—do the dirty work. That's why the bank didn't have her on surveillance.

The identity theft practically took over Trudy's life. "Within two months I had made a hundred and thirty-five phone calls," she recalled.

It didn't stop. Much later she received a call from Nordstrom's. "I was excited—I thought it was a job offer," she said. "But it was because this person had tried to open up an account in my name over the phone. To this day I still have a credit watch at all three credit bureaus, so that if anyone tries to open credit in my name, I must be called first. And I call them religiously every year to make sure no unauthorized activity has gone on in my name. It's something you have to do for fifteen, twenty years afterward. For example, eight years ago my son was buying a car and needed a cosigner. I said sure, I'll cosign. But Honda would not approve the loan because I have a block on it. I said oh, I have to go home and have them call me there at home. So to this day, if I were to want to go to Bloomingdale's and open an account, I couldn't do it."

The crook at Trudy's company was eventually arrested because she stole the identity of someone else at the company. "The bank called, and the coworker said hold her at the bank, I'm coming right over," Trudy said. "Sure enough, it was the woman in the accounting office. She had been doing this since she was fourteen years old, and she was arrested when she was in her twenties. And what she had done to us was nothing compared to what she had done in the past."

The thief's sister, as it turned out, was not at all involved.

Trudy said the emotional toll has been so enormous that she doesn't know how to quantify it. "You are so angry because it has cost so much time and energy, and you don't know when it's going to stop," she said. "Honestly, it's like opening a pillow at the top of a building, and the feathers just keep flying out and you can't control them and they're flying everywhere!"

After her bout with identity theft, Trudy returned to school and became a certified financial planner, and she's now a registered investment adviser. One of her first employers in her new capacity was a major financial institution whose name everyone knows. "When I was working there, I was astounded at the number of people there who have access to your information," she said.

The woman didn't go to jail for the theft against Trudy, but her criminal behavior eventually caught up with her, and she served two terms at the women's correctional facility in Bedford, New York. She was released on parole in October 2005. Will she strike again? This is a woman who has known one occupation in her life: identity theft. What do you think?

12

Write Your Company and Congressperson—Now!

My wife and I were on vacation in London. One day she ventured into a store and bought a sweater for $100. She handed the clerk her credit card, which had no balance on it and ample available credit. It was turned down. In the old days you would dial a number and straighten it out with an actual human being, but now trying to contact the issuer usually leads you to some lame automated response. The card had an 800 number to provide assistance. My wife asked if it would work in London. The clerk said, "I doubt it."

Back in our room we dialed the card company, paying for the call ourselves, to get to the bottom of things. When we finally wended our way to a live person, she said, "You should have told us you were going to London." In other words, the company had decided an identity thief was making the purchase, even though my wife was doing what millions of people do all the time, going someplace for a vacation.

My wife thought, Since when do I have to tell my credit card company when I'm going on vacation?

One of our sons was spending his summers at a school in China, and after that preposterous London incident, I made a point of notifying his credit card issuer of the dates when he would be there just to avoid more annoying headaches.

Now for my own embarrassing moment. I had a MasterCard with a credit limit of $15,000. I never charged more than about $3,000 in a given month, and I always paid the bill within thirty days. A short while ago, while I was in Washington, D.C., I stopped in at Nordstrom's and bought a pair of socks and a few other things. I charged them to the MasterCard, which at the time had a zero balance. The card was rejected. I asked the salesperson if he could find out why, and he miraculously managed to get a real person on the line. I asked to speak to her and said, "What's the problem?"

She replied, "Did you use your credit card at a pay phone sometime ago?"

I told her, "I may have. I don't usually do that, but I may have. What's that got to do with buying some socks?"

She said, "I need you to answer the question."

I told her again, "I'm not sure. What was the amount?"

She said, "How about you tell me?"

I eventually learned that an $8 phone call, which I probably made, had been charged to the card. But by then I was so exasperated, I said, "Let's forget about it, I'll use another card." When I got home, I cut my MasterCard in half and sent it with an explanatory letter to the issuer, telling them to cancel the card. I never heard a word back from them.

What's the moral of these stories? While it's clear that most companies are pretty apathetic about identity theft, a few have actually gotten so worked up over it that they've misguidedly gone too far in the other direction and as a result are making life doubly miserable for consumers. I don't want to see that happen. For instance, I've never had this sort of problem with my American Express card. We need to use our heads and strike a proper balance.

You've learned how to keep yourself from becoming the next victim of identity theft, and how to resolve things if you're victimized. But society and public officials have a responsibility as well, a big one. Congress and state legislatures need to provide consumers with more protection. So do the businesses that you so faithfully patronize. Remember, we're talking about a crime that takes place every four seconds. Its scope is a lot bigger than just one person.

A group that calls itself Artists Against 419, exasperated that law enforcement and companies don't do more about phishing scams, has actually been pursuing thieves on its own, a rare instance of a vigilante group aimed at white-collar crime. When one man found out that a department store had a videotape of the thief who had assumed his identity, he managed to obtain a copy of the tape and convince a local TV station to run it on the evening news. Several viewers recognized the man and called in to finger him.

But trying to round up crooks is dangerous work. People shouldn't have to do it themselves. The prevention tips I gave you are just Band-Aids. Systemic things also must happen, things that protect you without unduly inconveniencing you.

Ask This Question

First of all, every company in America, every government agency, every municipality, and every health care provider has to ask itself one simple question: What are we doing to protect the identity of our customers and our employees?

As a consumer, you've got to push them to get an answer to that question, because if they don't have the right answer, they're putting you at needless risk.

When I do consulting work for banks, I always say something like this: "You know, I was sitting out at your drive-in window, observing—I spent most of the afternoon out there. And I was watching Carol, who goes to high school until three in the afternoon and then works at the bank until seven. Every time a car pulled up to the drive-in, up on Carol's screen came the customer's name and address, Social Security number, date of birth, balance in his checking account, balance in his mutual fund account, and balance in his private banking account. Why would Carol need all that information? Why would you allow a part-time employee at that level access to that information? What are you doing to control and manage that information?"

At a bank that uses management identity software, the only thing that a teller would see is my name, address, and account number. All the other information—my date of birth and Social Security number—would be XXed out. If the teller needed my Social Security number, she would have to go on to her computer and then go to an officer of the bank, who would allow those XXs to disappear from the screen. And if the teller wanted my date of birth as well, she would have to leave the branch and go maybe 148 miles north to the operations center, where someone would have to allow those XXs to vanish. That's management identity software, made by companies like Novell for under $100,000.

A man recently recruited employees at four New Jersey banks to look up customer names and jot down their information, for which he paid $10 a name. He then sold them to others. He rounded up 750,000 names and made $4 million. He was able to do that because the banks had no internal controls. Software exists that can tell you, hey, there's suspicious activity at terminal 0761 in bank number 22 in Newark, but many banks are too cheap to install it.

When I do consulting work for hospitals, I always mention the switchboard operator. She's a volunteer who works one night a week. If I call and ask what room a patient is in, she will give me the room number, because it's in the computer. She can also give me the person's medical records.

I say to insurance agents, what are you doing to protect the identity of your customers? You probably have them on disks that your employees can copy. Do you think that's wise?

A lawyer I know who did wills had the misfortune of employing a dishonest bookkeeper, who took off with $35,000 of his money. That bothered him, but what bothered him much more was that she also took a computer disk on which she had downloaded all the names of his clients and their Social Security numbers, as well as their children's names and their identification numbers. The bookkeeper was caught, and he recouped the money but not the disk. The bookkeeper said she didn't know what happened to it. For all the lawyer knows, she unloaded it to a criminal ring.

Companies have to manage the identities of their customers, if for no other reason than liability. Who wants to be the insurance executive who is forced to get on TV and say that one of his employees stole all the names of the company's clients and now they've got to send out all these letters to everyone saying their information may have been jeopardized? And then if it is jeopardized, here come the lawsuits.

Identity theft, however, is easily prevented. The technology exists. In past years I have had the opportunity to talk to a group of three hundred chief financial officers of the Fortune 500 companies, organized by *CFO* magazine. One of the last times I lectured them, General Motors was in the audience, so I said, "General Motors, I just read where you're going to lay off twenty-five thousand employees. Let me ask you, when you lay off those employees, how long will it take the company to notify each department to remove their e-mail privileges, pass privileges, phone privileges, building access privileges, and card privileges?" The answer was nine months. I already knew that, because memos have to be sent out to the departments through layers of bureaucracy via the slow motions of a big corporation. I already knew that because when we talk to embezzlers and ask them, "You were fired by the company four months ago. How did you have access to this information?" they say, "Oh, yeah, they fired me, but I still had my e-mail privileges and I still had my phone privileges. Matter of fact, I'm still driving the fleet car they gave me. They haven't even called for that."

How is that possible, when the software to alleviate this problem exists from Computer Associates and Novell and many others for under $100,000? The proper answer to my question about how long it would take to delete all that information should have been, "About sixty seconds."

In the last year, how many personal digital assistants (PDAs) do you suppose were either lost or stolen from our nation's airports? Department of Justice records give the figure for people who filed a report with the airport police; I don't know how many people didn't contact the police. But the ones who did who had a PDA lost or stolen while they were in a U.S. airport totaled 253,000. What was on those PDAs? Personal and business information. Was it protected in any way? I doubt it.

Get References for the Janitor

No company hires a chief financial officer without undertaking a great deal of due diligence. But the cleaning person, working at night with hardly anyone else around, has access to trash that may contain sensitive information, file cabinets that have been left unlocked, documents that are resting on desks, and computers that haven't been turned off. Most companies don't check his references or even ask if he has any. They may be hiring him simply to clean up—but he could also easily clean the company out of personal information, including yours.

Corporations have to be urged to better screen job applicants and to restrict access to sensitive information. Anyone working in the payroll or personnel departments of a company would have continuous access to the private information of all employees, and they ought to be carefully screened. But if a company doesn't lock its file cabinets containing that information or protect computerized files, then anyone in the company has access to them. Anyone involved in processing expense accounts, including the secretary who first collects them, gets to look at personal data.

Many companies use temporary employees. Do they screen them? Does the agency that sent them screen them? Lots of businesses, especially smaller ones, outsource things like payroll services. What's the security policy of those outside vendors? Do they even have any? You don't even know the names of the people working there who are routinely handling your employees' private records. In early 2005 three former call center employees in India were arrested and accused of defrauding four Citibank account holders in New York of more than $300,000. You may trust your personal banker at Citibank. Have you ever met the call center guys in Mumbai?

Was It a Hammer or a Mop?

I've told you what you as a consumer ought to be doing to safeguard your computer and your Internet dealings, but you should also insist that the companies you interact with put in some heavy-duty online protection as well.

A study not long ago by Javelin Strategy & Research, a consulting firm specializing in Internet banking and payments, found that bank resolution services are preposterously slow. Only half of the banks in the study offered twenty-four-hour, seven-day-a-week account-shutoff services. Few banks were willing to send their customers e-mail alerts when unorthodox activity occurred in their accounts or when a pertinent piece of information like a phone number or address that was on file at the bank was changed. A number of the banks, in fact, said that they were reluctant to send out e-mails because they figured customers might think they were actually scams and delete them.

In 2005 banking regulators ordered banks by the end of 2006 to strengthen the log-on procedures for customers using online services. It specifically said that a user name and password alone are inadequate precautions, though it's not clear what regulators will accept to fortify security. You can be sure that banks will take the cheapest route they can get away with. You should insist that they take the most effective one.

Because messages can be intercepted, true authentication is impossible on the Internet. Knowing who is who will always be a formidable challenge. That's why my friend Ori Eisen of 41st Parameter likes to talk about how effective solutions ought to unite both overt and covert security measures. In a casino, he points out, you have the overt pit manager and the covert back room. The airport has overt security agents and covert air marshals. The army has the overt army and the covert special forces. Ori advocates, and I agree, that with online financial transactions the best approach is to use overt measures like passwords as well as covert features like risk management software and forensics tools.

A lot of products are floating around, but most of them are ineffective. Ori scoffs at them, and so do I. For instance, one idea being tried is the *shared secret*—a picture that is agreed upon between you and the bank and that appears each time you visit the bank's site, thereby confirming it's the genuine article and not an imposter site. It could be a picture of anything—a hammer or a hula dancer. They may seem easier to remember than a password, but call centers find themselves getting inquiries from bewildered consumers: How does this work? My wife's the joint account holder and she didn't know what the picture was. And as Ori points out, a thief could easily launch a phishing attack, stating, "Our image server crashed. Please pick a new image."

Some businesses have tried to get more adventurous with their "challenge" questions when verifying a consumer's identity, forging beyond the trusty old mother's maiden name or favorite pet. They try things such as, Who holds your mortgage? or, What kind of student loan do you have? or, When did you graduate from high school? The problem is, if you make it too difficult, not only might you frustrate the consumer, you could even help the identity thief. People's mortgages are sold again and again, and they may not even be certain which parent company owns it anymore. Does your wife know what year you graduated high school? And identity thieves are able to round up so much information on you that they're apt to be better equipped to answer some of these questions than you are.

In other words, in certain areas they know you better than you do. Some banks, in fact, get suspicious when someone answers every question correctly.

Banks are also experimenting with electronic tokens that provide numerical codes that change every thirty seconds and serve as a second password. They're very secure, but you have to carry them around, and there are maintenance costs. Another idea is to give users what look like bingo cards. When you enter your name and password to an account, you're asked to enter the numbers from various points on the card—such as A5, D6, and F4. But thieves can lure users to a fake site that tells them the number they entered is no good, and that way the thieves pick up workable numbers. You could have automated calls confirming a transaction. But what if wrong phone numbers are on your files, or you're making the transaction outside of your home and there's no one to take the call?

The approach I like is Ori's. He has developed a covert software product for financial institutions that, when you sign in, considers eighty different factors about the computer and thus determines the computer's fingerprint. These factors would be things such as whether the computer is different from the one the user usually uses or if it's in a high-risk country like Pakistan or whether there's an unusual time difference between the user's machine clock and that of the server—what's known as *time drift*. After instantaneously weighing these factors, it rates the likelihood of whether the user is you. It's a very effective solution. The beauty of this covert software is that it doesn't require any consumer action, so there can't be mistakes, and since the consumer doesn't have to do anything, there's no confusion or consumer resistance. It's very difficult for thieves to defeat.

It'll Be No Worse Than Going Shoeless at the Airport

So I favor companies taking some additional precautions, a few of which might mildly slow transactions, but not too many—and nothing like the ones my wife and I encountered when we had our shopping problems. And I'm against technology that intrudes excessively on privacy. Biometrics has become a hot area—the use of devices to identify people through physical features like the eye. These have been tried for building access and at ATMs. I think they're great for building entry and corporate and government identification cards but not for consumer commerce. I have concerns about people's privacy, and biometrics is going a little too far. We've surrendered enough privacy. I don't see why we should ask consumers to give up their irises.

But slowing things down a bit works for me. I know consumers insist on having everything fast and easy, and we've been spoiled by the time savings that technology has bestowed on us. Banks realize that customers don't like to be hassled. When people pull up to a drive-in window, they hate it when they're asked for their driver's license, especially when they've been banking there for twenty-five years. People don't like to be inconvenienced, and hassling customers less than your rivals is considered a real competitive advantage. Businesses know that the quicker they service someone, the more people they're likely to attract, and if that brings about a bit more crime, so be it.

Credit card companies have been reducing the amount of credit information they put on merchants' bills that could be too easily stolen. Still, lenders balk at restrictions that they say could curb the availability of credit at low rates. And card companies have few incentives or penalties to encourage them to keep more accurate and secure records.

The new thing for speedy shoppers is that when you go to the grocery store, you don't run your card through a slot and press "credit" or "debit" and enter a code. Instead, you have one of these "blink" cards that you just wave at the machine. The clerk doesn't know what you have in your hand. If he can even tell it's a card, he has no idea what it says on the face. He just knows you're out of there in two seconds. It's faster, but with no way to make sure the card is legitimate, it's going to lead to more crime. So I'm not a big fan of blink cards.

California and more than a dozen other states have enacted "freeze" laws that allow consumers to block access to their credit without permission. It's a trade-off. Banks howl that you can't then buy a car or a home and get approved for a mortgage in fifteen minutes over the phone, or apply for instant credit. If people freeze their credit, mortgage brokers say, it could take days to unfreeze it. What if you're hunting for a house in a hot market? Well, it seems Americans have too much credit, not too little. We've got debt galore and little savings. I don't see how slowing down the purchasing cycle a tad is so bad.

We really need to yield a little in some areas. Convenience at the cost of more crime is not appealing. Americans got all riled up when airport security was significantly tightened in the wake of September 11. The idea of removing your shoes and undergoing random searches made it seem like you could never get anywhere in a reasonable amount of time. Yet people discovered, in time, not only that it wasn't an undue hassle but that they were glad these procedures had been instituted because they felt safer. In fact, when the government relented on people carrying objects like small scissors, people were actually angry.

The same thing will likely happen with identity theft. People will quickly become accustomed to a few mild inconveniences here and there and then come to welcome them if they know that their finances are better protected.

Consumers should never be insulted if a salesperson asks for a piece of identification to verify who they are. If you're an honest person, why should you mind? The bottom line is, they're protecting you, and they're protecting the store. The less they're defrauded, the lower they can set their prices. We all benefit.

Tell Your Congressperson

Now that identity theft is our fastest-growing crime, our elected officials must own up to their responsibility as well. It's shameful that government doesn't do more. I've thought about what changes in the law could make a significant dent in this burgeoning crime, and I'd like to share them in the hope that you'll bring them to the attention of your public representatives. Groundswells of pressure are what prod legislators to take action and do the right thing. You're protecting yourself, your family, and your economy.

We need some new laws, but not too many, because excess legislation, especially the wrong kind, can backfire. Some of the new privacy laws that have been enacted might seem well intentioned, but they actually work in the criminals' favor, such as laws about companies not sharing information about ex-employees to new employers. I almost think that identity thieves must have their own lobby down in Washington pushing for some of these measures.

Toughen the Penalties

We still catch very few identity thieves, and many who are caught aren't prosecuted very aggressively. Still, the ones who are convicted should do some real jail time. Though some states have made scattered efforts to stiffen the penalties for identity theft crimes, they're still too light. In California in 2005 a defendant pleaded guilty to fifty-six counts of identity theft and was sentenced to a mere year in jail.

Imposing tough jail sentences may not discourage the hardened criminal, but a lot of the amateurs and part-timers may think twice before engaging in identity theft.

It was a step in the right direction when Zachary Keith Hill, 20, of Texas, was sentenced in 2004 to forty-six months in prison after pleading guilty to defrauding America Online and PayPal customers of $50,000 in online phishing schemes. You never used to see that before. And Howard Carmack, the so-called Buffalo Spammer, was convicted of sending more than 825 million junk e-mails and using stolen identities to block attempts to shut down his operation. He was sentenced to three and a half to seven years in prison, the first person prosecuted under New York State's identity theft legislation. To his credit, Eliot Spitzer, the New York attorney general who handled the case, has been quite outspoken about identity theft. It's no wonder—his own wife was a victim.

Rein in the Social Security Number

Social Security numbers have been around since 1936, when they were invented to track workers' earnings for Social Security benefits. Today you may not be able to leave home without your American Express card, but you can't exist without your Social Security number. And as we've seen, misuse of these all-important nine digits has become rampant. In 2006 there were approximately 230 million Social Security numbers held by individuals. Those are 230 million targets of opportunity for identity thieves.

There's no question that we need to cut way back on their usage and enact additional legislation that protects this number and sets penalties for its abuse. In 2004, state agencies in forty-one states and the District of Columbia displayed Social Security numbers in public records; this was true in 75 percent of U.S. counties. Most often the numbers are found in court and property records, stored either electronically or on microfiche or microfilm. Few state agencies make public records available on the Internet, but several hundred counties do. Why shouldn't it be zero counties? In 2004, according to the Government Accountability Office, something like 42 million Medicare cards displayed the holders' Social Security numbers. Eight million Department of Defense identification cards carried them. Seven million Department of Veterans Affairs identification cards contained them. Why?

Some states have passed measures that restrict companies, businesses, government agencies, and individuals from publicly displaying Social Security numbers, mailing them without precautions, and sending them over the Internet. California bars businesses, health care providers, and schools from publicly posting Social Security numbers, requiring them for access to products and services, printing the numbers on cards necessary for accessing products or services, compelling an individual to use his Social Security number to access a website unless a password is also required, and printing an individual's number on any materials that are mailed to the person.

New York State limits the use of these numbers in schools and colleges so they can't publicly display them. And federal agencies have begun to reduce their use. The Social Security Administration itself now truncates the numbers when it sends out its annual benefits statements.

But we need to go all the way. Uniform national legislation that applies to everyone who collects this number is imperative. For years now, a bill known as the Social Security Number Misuse Prevention Act has floated around the halls of Congress. Let's make it a law. By itself it won't cure this problem, but it will accomplish some valuable things.

In its latest rendition, the bill would prohibit the sale and display of Social Security numbers and limit their use by government agencies and businesses. While it would continue to allow business-to-business and business-to-government use of Social Security numbers, it would bar the sale and display of a number without the consent of the individual. The government would be prohibited from displaying these numbers on public records that get posted on the Internet or sent to the public through electronic means. It would restrict businesses' ability to require that customers provide their Social Security numbers, and it would forbid their insisting on it for consumers to purchase goods or services. To put some teeth in the law, it would authorize the Social Security Administration to issue penalties of as much as $5,000 against anyone who misuses a Social Security number. A thief who uses someone's number to assume his identity can get up to five years in prison.

Part of the problem is that we have allowed Social Security numbers to become so widespread that the cost of lowering their profile is going to be significant, but it's a cost that we must assume. The real benefit, of course, is to future generations, those who haven't yet been issued Social Security numbers. They are our children and this country's future.

Let Us Decide If It's Serious

I've told you about massive data heists, and the practice of low-level employees selling identities to criminal rings. California was the first state to require businesses to notify consumers when their personal information was compromised, and a couple of dozen states, at last count, now have similar legislation.

But consumers don't always get notified immediately. Sometimes it's weeks or months later. On New Year's Eve 2005 an employee of Providence Health System who lived near Portland, Oregon, left a case of computer disks containing 365,000 patient records in his van overnight in his driveway. Someone stole them. Oregon didn't have a notification law, but Providence did go ahead and alert the affected individuals. When? Nearly a month later. If you're going to wait that long, why even bother?

Some state laws that do mandate notification are equally ineffective because they're simply too hazy. In Washington State, for example, the law allows a company whose data has been stolen to decide if the breach is "serious" enough to require a mass notification. But what does *serious* mean? Lawyers could spend an eternity arguing that one.

In 2003 banking regulators issued new guidelines that require banks to tell customers if their personal information has been stolen or somehow compromised. These guidelines mimic state laws, but they have no force of law, and they also allow banks to decide when a consumer is at risk and should be advised of compromised data. A federal measure, the Data Accountability and Trust Act, that applies to all businesses that have data breaches takes the same lame approach, letting the company with the missing information decide if there is a need to notify customers. That's absurd. Why should the people who had the inadequate security to begin with decide if the screw-up was significant enough to tell the consumers who are actually put at risk? No CEO is going to announce a problem if he doesn't have to. The customer should be the one to say if something is significant or not and to be informed any time his information has fallen into the wrong hands. There should be a clear federal standard specifying just that.

Citizen Invasion

The 2003 federal Fair and Accurate Transaction Act contained a welcome stipulation, effective in June 2005, requiring that documents that include consumers' personal information must be destroyed—such as by shredding or burning—before being discarded. The law applies to consumers too, if you're handling someone else's personal information. Say you employ a babysitter or hire a contractor to renovate the kitchen, and you do a credit check on them; you can't just throw out the papers without shredding them. If you do a background check on a blind date, it's the same thing. If you don't destroy the records and you get caught, you could be fined.

I agree with this law as a valuable step, though I don't think I'd go too hard on people working the dating scene. Like everything else, though, it's not perfect and won't totally eliminate Dumpster diving. There's plenty of garbage not covered by the law that thieves can make productive use of. To take a far-fetched example, say you throw away a scrap of paper with a friend's phone number. No name, just the number. The law doesn't say you have to shred that, and why would you? Well, a thief can dig out that scrap and enter the number on a website that will return an address and sometimes a map showing the way to the person's home. The thief looks up the address in property records and gets the name, Social Security number, and more, and he's in business. Of course, he could start by picking a number out of the phone book, but you get the idea.

Another worthwhile move on the legislative front would be to require the police to take reports on identity thefts, not dismiss them because they're busy chasing loiterers or because the value of the crime doesn't meet their criteria. When I asked the people at Affinion, who have helped consumers resolve thousands of identity theft messes, what was the biggest obstacle they faced, they said that far and away it was indifference and outright resistance from the police. According to Affinion, police departments, especially those in bigger cities, often tell identity theft victims that they don't need to file a police report. Well, do they tell people who have been assaulted or whose cars have been stolen that they don't have to file a police report?

I understand the need to vigorously address violent crimes, but identity theft is wrecking a lot of lives, and the simple step of taking a police report often makes a big difference in enabling people to straighten out their credit. The FBI has become concerned enough that it has begun a program to urge all local police departments to report these crimes.

Still another worthwhile step would be to update the nation's death registry and implement precautions so that credit bureaus and government agencies don't wind up issuing benefits to the deceased. I know we're having enough problems protecting the living, but we've got to insulate the dead too from identity theft grave-robbers.

What about these proliferating digital dossiers floating through the ethereal world of the Internet, the ones compiled from public documents and the warranty questionnaires you filled out?

This is a sticky area, because when the Constitution was written, it was hard to envision things like ZabaSearch, that site I mentioned earlier where you could plug in an address and see satellite pictures of someone's home. It was hard to envision satellite cameras. Let's face it, it was hard to envision warranties.

The distribution of information happens in such stealthy and sophisticated ways today that the challenge of containing it without trampling on constitutional rights is immensely challenging.

When it comes to privacy, the federal and state constitutions generally protect it against invasion by the government. The problem today is invasion by other citizens and by companies. And of course the First Amendment protects the right of free speech, which includes publishing information. The combination of these two protections militates in favor of those who circulate information about you.

Some recent court cases underscore how ticklish it can be to suppress even personal information that could be used for crime. Consider *City of Kirkland v. Sheehan.* Bill Sheehan, who lives in the state of Washington, ran a website called justicefiles.org, on which he published a wealth of information about local police officers in Kirkland and in other Washington municipalities. What sort of information? How about their names, addresses, Social Security numbers, dates of birth, spouses' names—everything a crook needs. Not that Sheehan had crime in mind. He steadfastly maintained that his ambition was purely to ensure that police officers were publicly accountable. In other words, if an officer wasn't doing his job properly, you could call him at home, or go over and visit him after hours and give him a piece of your mind. I get the idea, but I'm not quite sure why you would need his Social Security number to point out his failings on the job.

The police department, naturally, was aghast. Officers said that this website put them, as well as their families, at greater risk, and that they had to take extra security measures to protect themselves.

The court didn't see it that way. It ruled that the site was protected by the First Amendment. It acknowledged that people might not like having their names and addresses, along with other personal information, publicized in that fashion, but it said that absent a credible threat of actual harm, the law shouldn't stop the dissemination of legally obtained information. It further noted that this dissemination could expose wrongdoers and facilitate peaceful and proper picketing of worksites and homes.

One significant victory was achieved. The single aspect of the dissemination to which the court objected was the publication of the officers' Social Security numbers, because, it said, they could be used improperly to track down and seize financial assets. The court ruled that this was a power vested in government and hence subject to constitutional restraint.

Given such rulings, as well as others, websites containing personal information are unlikely to be outright banned, and I'm not sure I would want that to happen, given the implications such an action might have in other areas of society. But why not at least extend protection to certain sensitive information? If we can safeguard medical information, we must be able to protect other personal information as well.

You Shouldn't Have a Criminal Record Forever

As I said earlier, sticking victims with criminal records is the scariest aspect of identity theft, because those records won't go away. And that's patently unfair.

Some states have taken stabs at correcting this injustice. California has an Identity Theft Registry, a database of confirmed victims of criminal ID theft. If the police detain someone who is in the registry, he or she can give the police a toll-free number and password to verify with the California Department of Justice that he or she is not the person wanted for a crime. It's staffed twenty-four hours a day. But the registry is not well known or understood, and few people have enrolled. States like Virginia and Ohio are issuing "identity theft passports" that victims can carry and show to the police. Again, they haven't been well publicized, and this document may become as easy to fake as any other form of identification.

These innovative steps in the right direction are not going to work unless they're accepted widely and heavily publicized. The real solution is that if you're able to prove indisputably that you did not commit a particular crime, then the crime should be expunged from your record, not just marked in some way as being questionable or otherwise resolved. It just shouldn't be there at all. And you should be able to eradicate it conveniently and inexpensively, not have to spend your life and a small fortune getting rid of it.

Who Pays If It's the Horse's Fault?

An online identity theft crime that occurred in 2004 raised some other troubling and complex issues. Joe Lopez, who operated a five-person ink and toner cartridge wholesaler in Miami, maintained an online business account with Bank of America. When he logged on to his account in early 2004, Lopez noticed to his dismay that an electronic transfer totaling more than $90,000 had been made from his account to a bank account in Latvia. Lopez did no business with anyone in Latvia. When he saw the withdrawal, as he later recounted, "I thought I was going to throw up." Within a day $20,000 of the Latvia deposit had been withdrawn in cash.

Lopez promptly notified Bank of America, which got the Secret

Service involved. They checked Lopez's personal computer and found the origin of the theft. A Trojan horse–transported virus known as CoreFlood had maneuvered its way past the antivirus software and firewall that Lopez had had in place to deflect attacks. The malicious software stole Lopez's user name and password and handed it to a data thief, who either used it himself or more likely sold it to the man in Latvia. It might have changed hands several times before settling in Latvia.

Bank of America refused to restore Lopez's stolen funds. It maintained that it had put in enough security, and in any event, the problem wasn't on the bank's computer but on Lopez's computer. It cited the Uniform Commercial Code that governs commercial contracts, which limits the bank's liability when it provides services to a business if it has instituted precautions. The bank said that it shouldn't be held responsible for infectious programs over which it has no control. In short, it told Lopez that he, not the bank, had screwed up.

A consumer would have been limited to a loss of $50 if he reported it quickly. Since Bank of America deemed Lopez a commercial customer, however, he was left in the lurch. He has sued the bank. Meanwhile he has abandoned his online bank account and transacts business using wire transfers.

You have to read your deposit agreement. But I think it's ridiculous for Bank of America to draw a distinction between a consumer account and a commercial one in a case like this. To suggest that it did nothing wrong is self-serving. I mean, why in the world did it permit such a sizable transaction to go through to a place like Latvia, a known site for identity fraud? We really need to get the law clarified.

Speak with Your Wallet

To a much greater extent, we must examine the consequences of the open-book society that has evolved, where anybody can know almost anything about anybody else. Yes, clever thieves will always be able to steal information, but we don't have to just hand it over to them. Barriers do reduce crime, and they certainly discourage the amateurs and low-level crooks who make up a good proportion of the identity theft universe.

So tell your congressperson and the companies that you patronize by using the most important powers you have at your disposal: your vote and your wallet. In endless instances credit issuers have blithely opened accounts in someone else's name when the thief offered a fabricated address, failed to spell the victim's name correctly, or even was a digit or two off on the Social Security number. Why deal with companies that function in such a sloppy fashion? Nothing gets the attention of a business faster than lost business, especially from a longtime and loyal customer.

13

───────── ✳ ─────────

Staying Two Steps Ahead (or Three)

Have you heard about the larcenous monkeys? It seems that Yale researchers succeeded in teaching a group of capuchin monkeys, those highly intelligent monkeys that organ grinders use, how to buy treats like grapes and Jell-O by exchanging metal tokens. In time, the monkeys also picked up the concept of value. When they learned that grapes were cheaper than bananas, they snubbed bananas and loaded up on grapes. Their understanding of economics struck me as quite impressive. But especially fascinating was the next step that the monkeys took. Presumably recognizing that you can never have too much money, the monkeys began to hide their tokens and fashioned counterfeit coins out of cucumbers that they tried to fool the researchers into accepting for fruit.

The instinct to cheat runs deep indeed, even in monkeys. I'm not happy about it, and we live today in an uncommonly unethical society. We just don't emphasize ethics the way we used to, and many people, especially young people, don't seem to appreciate the very essentials of right and wrong. As long as this remains true, identity

theft will intensify, in its tried and tested forms and in new variations as well. We don't know what identity thieves will do next, but
rest assured that they'll do something. Already they've begun to invade cell phones and personal digital assistants and steal data from
them. We're going to continue to see information swiped on a massive scale from companies and databases and sold not only in this
country but overseas to those who wish to assume the identity of
Americans. Even terrorists, I would think, would be able to slip into
someone's identity and get a job here and join a sleeper cell, because
it is so easy to do. I don't believe we've even begun to witness some
of the horrendous problems this crime will cause.

Every precautionary action we undertake to prevent identity
theft, therefore, has to take into account what could come next.
Crime is a full-time job for its practitioners. Every move to thwart it
has to anticipate the criminals' next move. You bolt one door, and the
thief comes in the other. You bolt that, and he uses the window. Lock
the windows, and he digs through the foundation.

Here's a good example. The average phishing site lasts only five
days before the crooks abandon it and move on to a new one. Why?
It usually takes about six days for law enforcement or security experts to shut it down. So the thieves head elsewhere just before they
hear the footsteps of the authorities closing in.

So you have to think two (if not three) steps ahead.

We Haven't Even Hit Intermission

As we contemplate this crime and how far it's come and how much
damage it's already wrought, we need to wake up to the fact that
identity theft is a drama still in its first act. More bleak acts are to
come as this crime continues to boom, unless the forces that can al-

ter the script work together for the collective good. We can't delude ourselves that criminals will just go away or take up pottery or something else to support themselves. Identity theft is too good a deal.

I hope that this book will serve as a call to arms. As more and more people with an evil bent notice identity theft's quick rewards, they too will make it their profession. I don't consider myself a paranoid person, and I certainly don't want you to become one. As a result of phishing attacks, overly cautious consumers are deleting real e-mails from eBay or their broker. I know someone who got a notification of a class-action settlement on behalf of purchasers of a stock that had tanked, but he threw it away rather than filling out the response because he was afraid it was a scam. That's not the way to live. If you're unsure of the authenticity of a communication, call the bank or merchant, getting the phone number from your monthly statement or any source that you know is legitimate.

People don't have to imagine an identity thief lurking on every street corner and burrowed in every letter and every e-mail. They just need to become a little smarter and a little more careful.

We're a very reactive society. We wait until there's a problem, and then we go and try to find some sort of solution to it. It's very easy for me to sell an identity theft program or a resolution program or a security program to someone who's already been victimized. They don't want it to happen again. But when I try to sell it to someone who's never had it happen to them, they say, well, that might not happen to me.

But do you have an insurance policy on your home? I ask. Do you pay the premiums every year? Have you ever had a fire or a flood? No, the person responds. Do you think you're going to have one? I ask. I don't think so, I'm told. Do you have life insurance? I ask. After all, you're still alive.

Obviously, when it comes to insurance, people are proactive. They think ahead and recognize that something awful could happen, and if the worst does happen, they want to have something in place to protect themselves. So why wouldn't they have the same philosophy about protecting their own financial well-being? Why wouldn't they care as much about guarding their own identity?

Let's at Least Slow It Down

You can't rely on government, you can't rely on law enforcement, and you can't rely on banks to protect you against identity theft. One identity thief, for instance, managed to access online loan applications at a bank out west. The bank called the FBI, which asked for the bank's entire disk of its loans so that it could investigate. The bank said, No way, we don't want this invasion to get out. So the FBI was forced to drop the investigation.

Here's a case that's even more absurd. In Troy, Ohio, state liquor-control agents trying to shut down a strip bar suspected of liquor violations set up a sting operation. They recruited a college student who had stripped in the past to get a job at the bar. As a cover, they gave her the actual Social Security number and driver's license number of another young woman in Cincinnati, who had no idea her identity was being assumed by a stripper. Ohio authorities maintained that, while this was a bit of a foul-up, under state law it was perfectly legal for them to borrow an identity in an investigation. What were they thinking? It was outrageous. The woman whose identity was used might find her "stripper career" included on future background checks. How's that *going* to look when she applies to be a librarian or a lawyer? As a further insult, she might even be assessed taxes for the earnings her impersonator made.

Let's face it, if stuff like this is going on, you must take steps to protect yourself. Technology exists to help, but you must commit to using it. And you must start thinking like a criminal, the way I do, and remember that a crook always looks for the easiest route to riches. Don't hand him a map.

I'm not foolish enough to think that we can stop identity theft altogether. I won't live to see that day, and I doubt anyone will. We don't cure crime in our societies the way that we manage to slay so many merciless diseases. We haven't been able to erase murder the way we have polio, to eradicate rape the way we have the plague. And I know we won't put identity theft in a coffin. No vaccines to inoculate you against it are percolating in the laboratories, and no bottle of pills will make the pain go away.

But we can slow it down—a lot. We can possibly transform it from a growth industry to one that is in steady decline. To do so we must take prevention more seriously and press businesses, legislators, and law enforcement to do the same.

We live busy lives, but this is a terrible problem. I don't want someone else to become Frank Abagnale, but I'm worried less about myself than about my children and yours as well as about our grandchildren and great-grandchildren. Remember, everyone is a potential victim.

I'll finish with one last story. An individual in the state of Washington, according to bill collectors, showed up at a medical clinic, received some treatment for a lumbar disk displacement, and was handed a prescription for some pain pills. He was a middle-aged man, but he had assumed the identity of someone else. He gave that name and its particulars, and no one questioned that he was who he said he was. The bill came due, $94, and when it wasn't paid, a notice eventually reached the people with whom the victim lived. They happened to be his parents. It wasn't a large bill, hardly worth mentioning alongside the much bigger sums we've seen, but it was a lot for him. Resources were tight. His career had yet to take root. He was three weeks old.

Acknowledgments

Many people helped in the preparation of this book, more than I could possibly mention, but I'd especially like to thank all the individuals who shared with me their encounters with identity theft. Innumerable law enforcement officers, businessmen, government agencies, consumer organizations, and ordinary citizens kindly provided useful information, for which I'm grateful. Some of them are mentioned by name in the book, while others, particularly those who were victimized, have preferred to remain anonymous.

My sincere thanks, as well, to the more than three thousand companies and associations that have allowed me to work with them, particularly the Standard Register Company, the Affinion Group, Novell, Sanford Uni-ball, Leigh-Mardon-Australia, the Discover Network, and Staples, Inc. I'm extremely grateful to Ori Eisen for sharing his wisdom on technologies to prevent this crime.

I am indebted to all the talented men and women of the Federal Bureau of Investigation for supporting me and affording me the privilege of teaching at the FBI Academy and of assisting with programs in the bureau's field offices. Without them, none of what I do today could be possible.

Once again, I owe a debt of gratitude to Charlie Conrad and his colleagues at Broadway Books for their wisdom and for so skillfully shepherding this project from manuscript to publication. I certainly appreciate David Drake's key role in that process. My thanks, as well, to Andrew Blauner, my literary agent, for his steadfast support.

Finally, I could never have written this book without the invaluable assistance of Sonny Kleinfield and Susan Saiter, and I thank them for their contribution.

About the Author

Courtesy of the author

FRANK W. ABAGNALE is the author of the best-selling memoir *Catch Me If You Can* as well as *The Art of the Steal.* He works closely with the FBI and corporations around the world as an expert on counterfeiting and secure documents. He lives in the Midwest with his wife and is the father of three sons.